Labor in the Global Digital Economy

Labor in the Global Digital Economy

The Cybertariat Comes of Age

Ursula Huws

AAKAR

Labor in the Global Digital Economy: The Cybertariat Comes of Age
Ursula Huws

First Published in India 2015
Reprinted 2026

ISBN 978-93-5002-352-5

Published in agreement with Monthly Review Press, New York for publication and sale only in South Asia.

Published by
AAKAR BOOKS
28 E Pocket IV, Mayur Vihar Phase I
Delhi 110 091, India
www.aakarbooks.com

Printed at
D.K. Fine Art Press, Delhi

Contents

Introduction

In 2003, *Monthly Review Press* published a collection of my essays dating back to the late 1970s under the title *The Making of a Cybertariat: Virtual Work in a Real World.* This collection continues where that one left off, bringing together essays written between 2006 and 2013, a tumultuous period in the history of capitalism and the organization of labor.

In the earlier collection, one of my central themes was capitalism's extraordinary ability to survive the crises that periodically threaten to destroy it by generating new commodities. Just at the point when its logic of expansion seems destined to generate a saturation of markets and a consequent crisis of profitability, it finds fresh areas of life to bring within its scope, generating new forms of production of new goods and services for which new markets can be created. These phases are often associated with the diffusion of new technologies. In the early twentieth century, for instance, the spread of electricity gave rise to a wave of new commodity development based on domestic labor (such as vacuum cleaners, washing machines, and refrigerators) or entertainment (such as radios, film projectors, or phonographs and the films and records that provided them with content). In the process novel forms of production were generated, but so too were novel forms of consumption. While new kinds of paid work were created, domestic labor was increasingly transformed into what I termed "consumption work," sucking ever more activities out of the private sphere of direct interpersonal interaction and bringing them into a public marketplace. The more workers become dependent on these new commodities to survive from one day to the next, the greater their need for a source of income to pay for them, tightening capitalism's grasp on their lives still further. Yet such innovations are, on the whole, adopted willingly and enthusiastically. There is an almost irresistible appeal in their novelty, modernity, and convenience, their increasing cheapness, the promise they hold out of saving time and labor, and the lure of possessing something that was previously a luxury only the rich could afford. And those who do resist, positioning themselves thereby as old-fashioned, technologically inept, conservative, or even Luddite, quickly find that so many features of social and economic life are designed on the assumption that everyone now has these new commodities that survival without them becomes ever more difficult. The last volume charted some of the impacts of these developments on labor, both paid and unpaid, in a context in which capitalism was not only expanding in terms of the areas of life it embraced, but also in its geographical scope.

We have now entered a period, I argue here, when new waves of commodification set in motion in earlier periods are reaching maturity. The new commodities have been generated by drawing into the market even more aspects of life that were previously outside the money economy, or at least that part of it that generates a profit for capitalists. Several such fields of accumulation have now emerged, each with a different method of commodity genesis, forming the basis of new economic sectors and exerting distinctive impacts on daily life, including labor and consumption. They include biology, art and culture, public services, and sociality.

I use the term "biology" to refer to the way that life itself, in the form of plants and animals and the DNA that makes them up, is exploited to produce commodities such as new drugs and genetically engineered forms of food. This is a vast and expanding field, with huge implications for many aspects of life. I mention it only in passing and do not go into detail here, because, although I believe it to be very important, I have done no research in this area and have little to add to the interesting debates taking place elsewhere. I concentrate now on three other fields: art and culture, public services, and sociality.

The commodification of art and culture is the continuation of a process with a long history. Artistic work has been paid labor for centuries, and cultural commodities also have a long pedigree, produced under a variety of social and contractual conditions. What has changed in recent years has been the scale of their incorporation into capitalist productive relations, the concentration of capital in these sectors, and the introduction of a global division of labor into the production of cultural commodities. The concentration of ownership among a few transnational companies has been encouraged by technological developments that have enabled a convergence between activities that were formerly dispersed across different industries. Newspaper and book publishing, television, film, record, and games production, and other "content-generating" industries have merged seamlessly with each other and with distribution companies and infrastructure providers to create corporate behemoths that bestraddle a wide range of activities, interlinking the efforts of "creative" workers with many other technical, clerical, managerial, and service workers across the globe in ever-changing configurations. I analyze creative work at greater length in chapter 5.

In the late twentieth century, the income and working conditions of writers, film-makers, musicians were largely dictated by the terms they could negotiate with vertically organized film companies, record companies, and publishers whose profits were directly linked to the sale or distribution of commodities such as films, records, CDs, books, and magazines. Now the markets are increasingly dominated by companies that produce hardware (such as Amazon's Kindle, or Apple's iPhone) alongside distributing the content for them (in the form of eBooks or iTunes). In the process of these sectoral shifts of power, creative workers have been reconstituted as "content producers" for products made by other industries. This has several impacts. It links their work more directly with that of other "knowledge workers," such as software developers, and, increasingly, requires them to take on tasks previously carried out by others (such as copy editors, typesetters, designers, recording technicians, camera operators, and the like). It also loosens their hold on their intellectual property. As the twentieth century vertically integrated companies struggle to adapt to the new market conditions, the main asset they have to exploit—the output of these creative workers—becomes something to be resold in multiple forms on multiple platforms for different audiences. Having lost control, in many cases, of the final delivery of these items to the public, they are forced to sell them to intermediary distributors and settle for a smaller share of the profit, with the financial squeeze transferred to the workers. For companies like Amazon or Apple, if sales of eBooks or iTunes cease to become ends in themselves and become simply means to sell more Kindles or iPhones, then the companies' interests cease to lie in the maximization of the profit from any given title, but only in increasing the overall quantity of sales across all titles in order to expand the choice available to hardware users, to encourage more sales of these gadgets. This drastically changes the economics of media industries, removing bargaining power from creative workers and driving down the earnings of the majority (though enabling a minority of stars to flourish). Even those artistic workers who strive to work in traditional ways, outside the market, find themselves in practice increasingly having to beg and brag to large corporations or bureaucracies for the access to the resources that will allow them to do so. I discuss this culture of begging and bragging in chapter 3.

The commodification of public services has followed a rather different route, although there are strong connections and overlaps between this and the commodification of cultural activities because of the strong cultural content of public services such as education. The development of public services, delivered by a paid workforce of government employees, was an important feature of the twentieth century, both in communist countries, where it was the normative model for all employment, and in developed capitalist economies, where welfare states—and the public employment associated with them—arose and expanded, especially in the period following the Second World War, in an accommodation between the demands of labor and the requirements of capital, an accommodation that took different forms in different contexts in its specific features. Though undoubtedly playing a functional role for capital, in terms of reproducing the workforce, these state-provided services can also be seen as representing a victory for organized workers, who had long campaigned for such things as pensions, free education, health services, unemployment, and sickness benefits on behalf of the working class as a whole. As such, public services represent a portion of what labor has managed to claw back from capital, reflected in terminology such as the "social wage." Opening up these services as a new arena for capital accumulation has far-reaching and multidimensional impacts. In formerly communist countries after 1989, this reappropriation was often achieved by a simple grab, creating the basis for new kleptocratic oligarchies. Elsewhere, it was a subtler, but equally pernicious, process, achieved partly through outright privatization but increasingly through a creeping process of outsourcing, function by function, department by department, region by region, to a new breed of multinational companies waxing fat on the proceeds, and able to use their global spread not only to draw on cheap sources of labor but also to minimize the amount of tax they pay to the governments that so obligingly provide them with the material from which they make their profits. Chapter 6 traces the development of the commodification of public services, linking it to the global restructuring of value chains that is described in earlier chapters.

It is perhaps my next category of new commodification, sociality, that is the most mind-boggling in its implications when considered as the basis of new commodities and new industries. The human needs to flirt and talk and share jokes and commiserate and keep in touch with friends and family must have seemed to our ancestors to be as basic as the needs for animals to nuzzle up to one another. Surely, they would have thought, these must be impervious to the hard cold laws of capitalism; how could they possibly provide a source for corporate profit? I suspect that many people still cling to an idea that their personal relationships lie in a private realm of affect and authenticity beyond the reach of the market. Yet the most cursory glance at almost any group of people in almost any social situation in the developed world shows how illusory such notions now are.

Here are just four snapshots drawn, more or less at random, from my own recent observations.

The first snapshot is of a group of schoolchildren walking down the street together, speaking animatedly and at high volume, not to each other, but to people who are absent. Most obviously, some mobile phone company is gaining a tariff for every minute of their communication which would be free if they chose instead to speak directly to each other. Other companies are no doubt also benefiting from their online activities: social media companies, and the companies that advertise on them, for instance. But there is also the matter of the hardware itself. The child who has the latest smartphone is able to flaunt this badge of social status. Those who do not (the children whose parents are unemployed, single parents, recently arrived immigrants, or otherwise unable or unwilling to provide them) are rendered vulnerable to a sense of inadequacy and exclusion in addition to those that are already present under advanced consumer capitalism (such as having the wrong brand of shoes or clothing). The colonization of their sociality by the market has not only generated a new source of profit-making but has also helped to drive wedges into the fabric of their social lives, undermining the basis for future solidarities.

My second snapshot is of five people sitting together around a café table, two of them expertly texting, one speaking on a phone complaining about the poor quality of the signal, another using his phone to photograph his surroundings, and the fourth looking exasperatedly at the menu. None seem to be enjoying themselves. Instead of using the rich and subtle multi-sensorial potentialities of direct interpersonal contact, they are choosing restricted channels for their communications: the verbally impoverished telegraphese of SMS messages, the mangled signals of shouted words. Once again, the corporate profits are accruing in tandem with deterioration in the quality of interpersonal social interaction.

My third snapshot is of a crowded London bus, with a cacophony of phone conversations in several languages, some loud and confrontational, some revealingly intimate, some so banal as to seem entirely unnecessary, with almost the character of a nervous tic, as though the caller cannot bear to be idle for a moment and being in communication gives an illusion of activity: "I'm on the bus. Yes, the number 73. I left work fifteen minutes ago. Yes, I'll be there in about twenty minutes. No, nothing special." Many of those who are not speaking on their phones are seated with earphones clamped to their ears, attached to various electronic devices they are fingering. This enables them to avoid interaction with the frailer people to whom, according to the signs above their heads, they should be offering their seats. The bus is no longer, as it was in the past, a place for unexpected encounters, the sharing of jokes with strangers, or a communication to lighten the spirits of a lonely person for whom this might be the only social contact of the day. While on the one hand the private intimacies of the bedroom or kitchen are yelled out indiscriminately to the world, on the other the strangers who share the same immediate social space are ignored, glared at, or rejected as communication partners. The relationship between the private and the public seems to have been turned inside out. But all the while a stream of income is being generated for the global communications companies.

My fourth and final snapshot is of a conference session, with four people on a platform, from three continents, one of whom is chairing, one speaking, and the other two looking down at their laptops or iPads; most of the audience are doing the same, several obviously working their way through their email, with almost no eye contact between any of them, despite the fact that most have traveled considerable distances (using up a lot of jet fuel in the process) to be together in person. In each case, there is a rejection of free communication by direct voice or touch or glance in favor of electronically mediated conversation. The (no doubt jet-lagged) speakers are dully reading prepared papers, which anyone in the audience could have read elsewhere on paper or from a range of different devices. Some may even be doing precisely that at this moment, giving themselves time to prepare a suitably self-positioning intervention when the speaker has finished. The point of being there seems to be to establish a record for future job applications that a paper has been presented rather than any desire for real dialogue. The expensive charade seems to be producing very little in the way of direct interaction, though of course some of this might take place in the bar later, among those who are not so time-poor that they retreat instead to their hotel rooms to catch up with their emails, call their long-suffering families, or write the next conference paper.

Where is the presence of capitalism in all this? Everywhere! It benefits, most obviously, from the physical devices—the mobile phones, tablets, laptops, iPads, and the accessories that have to be purchased to charge them and connect them to each other or to our persons. The manufacturers whose brands are displayed on them represent the tip of an iceberg of labor encompassing the miners who extract the minerals that are their raw materials, the factory workers who assemble them, transport workers, warehouse workers, service workers, software engineers, call center workers, and many more. Then there is the infrastructure: the (very solid) satellites and cables and Wi-Fi routers that enable all this seemingly evanescent digital content to be accessible so invisibly across the airwaves; and the electrical grid supplying the power without which none of it could run. Again, these require the labor of a large number of workers, employed by a large number of companies to do many things including extract coal and oil, erect windmills, run power stations, make cables, and create channels for them to be laid under our roads and fields and oceans. Not to mention the scientists who design the rockets that are blasted into space to put the satellites into orbit. Some of these industries already existed prior to the development of information and communications technologies, of course, but their markets have grown enormously as a result of the spread of digital communications. In relation to energy, for instance, it was estimated that using Information and Communication Technologies (ICTs) consumed between 930[1] and 1,500[2] billion kilowatt hours in 2013.

Furthermore, each of these electronically mediated interactions is generating income for the multinational corporations that run the telecommunications services. Social communication now involves, in effect, the payment of a tithe to these companies by every person around the world with a mobile phone contract or an Internet connection in the home—a number that continues to grow exponentially. In addition to generating income from call and broadband charges, communicating over a telecommunications network using a digital device also produces revenue for many other corporations, large and small, such as those that design operating systems or applications or charge users for playing online games. This is not all. When human sociality is mediated by telecommunications systems, it leaves digital traces wherever it goes, traces that can be mined to generate data that enable advertising to be targeted with ever-greater accuracy. The Internet is thus constituted as a vast virtual shopping mall, with its users bombarded with a constant stream of advertising, preying on their most personal vulnerabilities. So accustomed are most of us to these ever-present advertising messages that it is easy to forget how deeply damaging they are. From early childhood, most people are now told, hundreds of times a day, that they are fat, ugly, undesirable, vile-smelling, laughably old-fashioned, endowed with breasts or penises that are the wrong size or of the wrong degree of firmness, and that they are never likely to be popular unless they purchase whatever commodity is on offer to provide the magic fix for this problem. By such means even companies producing the most non-virtual of material products are able to intensify their sales, managing to sell more of their products even when the markets for them might be thought already saturated. This is partly achieved by persuading people to use more of them, for instance to take several showers a day, using even more shower gel and shampoo, partly by encouraging a kind of collective bulimia of consumption, whereby products are obsessively bought, then quickly discarded and replaced, and partly by developing new products. This is, of course, in addition to the traditional forms of expansion based on finding virgin consumers to sell to in developing economies.

Online advertising is more intense, and better targeted, than anything that went before, but there is nothing intrinsically new about this form of selling, though it is undoubtedly the case that the Internet has enabled some multinational corporations to grow, consolidate, and extend their global reach to a remarkable degree. A less expected development of the commodification of sociality has been the phenomenal rise of companies that make their profits by extracting rent both from these commodity-producing companies and from their customers online, on the one hand providing the means for web users to communicate with each other (for instance using Facebook or Googlemail) and on the other persuading them to deliver up their most intimate secrets to the advertisers to enable their vulnerabilities to be exploited. I discuss the ways that value is generated online in greater detail in chapter 7.

Taking into account the vast new fields of commodification I have summarized here, and others I have not described in detail, it is not surprising that capitalism does not only survive its periodic crises, but emerges from each with renewed vigor, and a new armory of resources to bring to reestablishing its relationship with labor on fresh terms.

To understand what is changing in this relationship between capital and labor it is perhaps useful to look back to earlier periods. Any attempt to periodize history is of course fraught with risk. Focusing attention on a moment of rupture usually involves ignoring the many continuities that remain constant in the background and, since the seeds of each new phenomenon lie in the preceding period, it is rare for the exact moment of its birth to be datable precisely. Nevertheless, it is hard to deny that there are certain moments when new phenomena reach a critical mass that brings qualitative, as well as quantitative change. Social and economic changes, and the technological innovations with which they are so often intimately entangled, tend to follow a similar path. Rare experiments by pioneers or elites are followed by broader voluntary uptake, which is in turn followed by mass adoption leading ultimately to a situation where the usage of whatever it is (school attendance, electricity, the telephone, prepackaged food) is so taken for granted that social institutions and policies are designed on the basis that they are universal practices.

I contend that we are now living in a period in which a series of mutually reinforcing economic, political, and technological factors have brought about just such a sea change in the character of work. I do not wish to suggest here that *all* work has changed. Far from it. My argument is, rather, that a range of features of work that were regarded in previous periods as exceptional or unusual are now taken for granted by a growing proportion of the population and, in the process, expectations of what "normal" working behavior should be have also been transformed. This situation has not come about overnight. Its origins can be traced back to earlier periods, when the dominant models were different. Oversimplifying considerably (there are, of course, many exceptions and counterexamples), I argue here that there have been three such periods since the end of the Second World War and that we are now in a fourth. Some of the changes that took place over this period are further discussed in chapter 1.

The first of these periods, extending approximately from 1945 to 1973, saw the creation of what has been variously termed the "postwar Keynesian welfare state,"[3] "the Golden Age of Capitalism,"[4] "Fordism,"[5] or "Les Trente Glorieuses."[6] In the developed capitalist economies of the West, and some developing ones, this was a period of national economic plans, often developed within tripartite structures between national governments, employers, and trade unions. Although some firms were already multinationals during this period, economies were dominated by national (sometimes nationalized) corporations willing to negotiate compromises at a national level. This enabled governments, at least in some countries, to use early twentieth-century antitrust laws to exercise some sort of control over corporate behavior. Many industries were still dependent on sector-specific or company-specific skills, which gave labor a degree of bargaining power in particular industries or regions. Even more important, the Cold War created a strong incentive for special deals with labor to be struck. Hovering in the background, in North America, Western Europe, and elsewhere, was a real fear that if concessions were not made to the trade unions workers would turn to communism. It was during this period that certain expectations were established, at least for skilled white male workers, that employers should provide continuous, contractually formalized employment, offering regular holidays, sick pay, pensions, and prospects of advancement. This was by no means a reality for many workers, particularly women, people from ethnic minorities, and those in low-skilled occupations. But even if it was not a universal reality, it was seen as a legitimate aspiration not only in developed economies but in developing ones, where "development" was often imagined in terms of achieving a formal labor market characterized by full-time, permanent jobs, just like those in the West. Implicit in this labor market model was a family model, equally at variance with reality for many workers: the full-time worker was conceived as a male breadwinner, the head of a dependent household where others carried out the unpaid reproductive labor.

The oil crisis of 1973 can be seen as marking the end of this period and the beginning of the next, dating approximately from the mid-1970s to the end of the 1980s. Now, in a context of declining profitability, conflicts between employers and labor were sharpened and employers made increasing use of migrant workers and women (many working part-time) to fill lower-paid positions. Waves of mergers and acquisitions brought an increasing concentration of capital, and the multinational companies that resulted began to relocate manufacturing work to lower-wage countries, sometimes to specially designated Export Processing Zones where they were protected from environmental and safety legislation and offered certain tax advantages. National and regional governments, with dwindling power to regulate these companies, increasingly found themselves forced into competition to attract foreign direct investment, offering subsidies and other inducements to lure such prizes as a major auto plant to their territory. Meanwhile, the development of information technologies made it possible to simplify and standardize many labor processes, including in-service industries, undermining the bargaining power of some traditionally well-organized groups of workers, while also opening up new areas of employment for others. Deindustrialization brought structural unemployment to some regions, but the model of the "job for life" was still in contention. In the global West, unions remained strong in many regions, with losses in some fields offset by gains in others, particularly in the public sector and in service industries employing large numbers of women and minorities, who were increasingly vocal in pursuit of equality and new rights. Although a discourse about "atypical" employment began to emerge, jobs were, on the whole, still regarded as subject to formal regulation and contractual negotiation.

The symbolic beginning of the next phase can be dated to the fall of the Berlin Wall in 1989, but this highly charged moment coincided with a number of other political, economic, and technological developments that taken together brought about a scale of change justifying the designation of the next period, running approximately from 1990 to the mid-2000s, as another distinct era in employment relations. It was not just that the ending of the Cold War opened up the whole world as a potential field of accumulation for capital (while removing the fear that workers would abscond en masse to communism). This was buttressed by a general wave of deregulation, opening up free trade in goods and services and enabling unhindered flows of capital, intellectual property, and information across national borders throughout the world. Deregulation did not only apply to trade restrictions. Neoliberal regimes went on the offensive against trade unions, reducing employment protection and embarking on a process of privatization that began to open up the public sector as a new field of profitmaking.[7] Meanwhile, the information technologies that had begun to be introduced in the previous period reached critical mass, becoming cheaper and more ubiquitous. The productive potential opened up by digitization had been limited when its scope was mainly confined to particular computers in particular locations, but this was greatly enhanced when Information Technology (IT) was harnessed to telecommunications (ICT), enabling these individual computers to be linked to one another in increasingly seamless ways and their contents exchanged as rapidly as the capacity of the telecommunications infrastructure would allow. In 1992, the International Telecommunications Union (ITU) was formed, initiating an era of rapid deregulation and upgrading of telecommunications networks around the world, with a lowering of prices for some services and the launch of new ones, such as mobile telephony. The same year marked the first use of SMS messaging and the launch of the World Wide Web, which grew from fifty web servers in January 1993 to over 500 by October of that year.[8] In 1992 India removed the barriers that had prevented it from exporting software, opening up the potential for large-scale remote processing of digitized information.

The stage was thus set for the development of a global division of labor in information-processing work, echoing that which had begun to appear in manufacturing work in the previous period. This did not develop overnight, of course. There were many hiccups along the way. Early adopters of ICT-enabled offshore outsourcing encountered many problems, including those created by technical incompatibilities between different systems, inadequate infrastructure, communication problems, cultural differences, resistance by workers and managers, and the difficulty of standardizing complex processes that drew strongly on workers' tacit knowledge. Although the teaching of global languages and computer skills was actively pushed by a range of national and international bodies, it took time for these to spread. Nevertheless, the 1990s saw a steady growth in offshore outsourcing to developing regions in India and other parts of Asia and Latin America, helped not only by a general growth in delocalizable services, such as call centers, but also by the need for large-scale routine software engineering associated with such activities as the conversion of European currencies to the euro, the explosive expansion of the Internet, and the much-hyped "Millennium Bug." Some of these developments and their implications for city life are explored in chapter 2.

Meanwhile, this was a period both of frenetic growth and of economic instability. The "Asian Tiger" economies rose and crashed in the mid-1990s and at the end of the decade the dot-com bubble ballooned and burst. Nevertheless, use of ICTs spread inexorably around the globe and new industries and companies emerged based on their use. These included the "new breed of multinationals," as they were described by UNCTAD in 2004,[9] specializing in the provision of outsourced business services, global telecommunications providers, media conglomerates, and the beginnings of the giant corporations that now dominate the Internet. Chapter 4 sets out an explanatory framework for the development of this new global division of labor, rooted in classical political economy.

It was toward the end of this period that telemediated digital communications became part of the taken-for-granted normality of daily life (just as using the telephone had become normalized a half century earlier). While consumers got used to ordering goods online and accessing support via call centers, managers began to be asked by their directors why they had not considered outsourcing as a solution to reducing their costs. More subtly, the idea of work as something unbounded and "virtual" began to take root. With the increasing use of email (which could be checked from any location), the fixed boundaries between home and work were eroded. And with workers increasingly paid, and managed, by results and requirements for "flexibility" ever more likely to be written into job descriptions, the hours spent formally working were less likely to be counted. Young people were increasingly expected to undertake unpaid "work experience" before entering the labor market. Others began to use the Internet for activities that hovered ambiguously between "work" and "play." Almost invisibly, many of the parameters that had defined a job in earlier periods were dissolving away.

This period can be thought of as ending abruptly with the global financial crisis of 2007–8. In its aftermath the employment landscape was suddenly very different. The combination of draconian austerity measures with unemployment levels higher than at any time since the Great Depression of the 1930s now presented young people with few options but to accept whatever was on offer to them in the labor market. This was a generation that had grown up taking ICTs for granted as an everyday part of life, as familiar with social media, online games, and SMS messaging as their grandparents were with pen and paper. And, even if the work they were applying for was manual or face-to-face, they were expected to use ICTs for such things as filling in application forms and communicating with employers. ICTs had, in other words, become part of the taken-for-granted environment of *all* work. The dissolution of clear boundaries between work and non-work and the erosion of formal rules governing work, while still not universal in existing jobs, was becoming ever more prevalent in those that were newly created. This blurriness of boundaries was by no means exclusive to online work, but a generation already primed to accept the interpenetration of "fun," "education," and the normal business of life online was ill-equipped to dispute such slippages in relation to boundaries between these activities and work in other spheres.

After the crisis, it was as though the world had woken up to a fundamentally changed reality, one in which a range of trends that had been evident, though not dominant, in the previous period had, almost overnight, become the new normality. The new landscape is dominated by transnational corporations to an unprecedented degree. But these corporations differ in several respects from earlier periods. A glance at the rankings of the world's top companies gives evidence of some of these trends. First, the global corporate environment is no longer almost exclusively dominated by the United States, Europe, and Japan. Companies based in economies formerly classed as developing play an increasingly important role in shaping the contours of the global economy, and hence global labor markets. No less than sixty-one of the Fortune 500 countries are now based in China.[10] The Fortune 500 ranking is based on revenues, which might be regarded as overstating their importance. However, even in the *Financial Times* (*FT*) ranking, which is based on market value, twenty-three of the top 500 companies are based in China, twelve in India, ten in Brazil, eight in Russia, and five in Mexico.[11] Forbes ranked three Chinese companies in the global top ten in 2013.[12]

Furthermore, many of these international companies operate in fields that were formerly seen as national in scope. These include formerly nationalized utilities (including telecoms, energy, water, and postal services) and public services such as health, education, and back-office services supplied to public administration. They also include the mass media, formerly the preserve of national broadcasting companies, nationally or regionally based newspapers, and small or medium-sized publishing companies. All of these fields, and many others, including retail chains, are now dominated by huge conglomerates. The *FT*'s top 500 companies include seventeen global mobile telephone companies and fifteen fixed-line ones, fifteen giant media companies, fifteen software and computing companies, and eleven health care companies, all global in scope. Companies providing outsourced services or labor-only subcontracting have also made it into the top rankings. Accenture is number 385 in the Fortune 500 list and Addeco is number 443.

Young people entering the labor market are not only much more likely than in the past to find themselves working for one of these global behemoths; they also do so in direct competition with similarly qualified workers from across the globe. Regardless of where they are located, they have been reconstituted as part of a global reserve army of labor, which can be accessed by footloose employers in two distinct ways: offshoring or migration.[13] The bargaining power of these workers vis-à-vis these employers is thereby dramatically reduced in comparison to their predecessors in earlier periods, and their lives, both as workers and as consumers, are increasingly shaped by these corporations, often in ways that the local state has little power to intervene in.

These developments are not, of course, without their contradictions. It would be far too simplistic to suggest a single universal trend—a global race to the bottom unmediated by any contrary trends. Such contradictions can be found at work at many levels: between nation-states, between companies, between states and companies, between companies and workers, and within each of these constituencies. Here I summarize just a few examples.

At the level of national governments, the mobility of capital has introduced new forms of competition between countries to attract foreign direct investment. It is also clear that the internationalization of capital and globalization of markets has brought about a dramatic reduction in the ability of any given national government to exercise the kinds of control over capital that were in place, at least in the more powerful imperialist nations, at the beginning of the twentieth century. I refer here to things like the antitrust laws that enabled states to break up monopolies, and the ability of governments to tax corporations. Since then a number of supranational bodies have been set up to manage the global economy, including the World Trade Organization,

International Monetary Fund, World Bank, and the executive bodies of the large trading blocs such as the European Union (EU), North American Free Trade Area (NAFTA), Association of Southeast Asian Nations (ASEAN), and Mercado Común del Sur (MERCOSUR, the Common Market of South America). These have succeeded in driving through regulations that force open national markets and enable the free flow of capital, intellectual property, and trade in goods and social services. However, they have markedly failed either to control the development of global monopolies or to prevent transnational corporations from basing their holding companies in tax havens and using transfer pricing and other mechanisms to avoid the payment of tax in the countries in which they operate. The willingness of national governments to privatize their assets and outsource their public services to profit-making corporations has also resulted in a loss of control of the management of these state services, not only allowing the profits to leak outside national borders but also making it possible for these companies to make use of a global division of labor to provide them, resulting in the loss of jobs for national citizens, with a resulting drain on national resources. These developments taken together are producing a crisis of legitimacy for governments in at least some states, in the process opening up a space for alternative political demands.

At the level of companies, globalization also opens up huge contradictions. The simplification of labor processes and procedures, leading to the production of highly standardized products in locations with low regulation, dubious attitudes to intellectual property, and cheap labor, opens up access to the market to new companies, unencumbered with any legacy costs or commitments to the development of new products. This produces a competitive environment in which profits are dramatically squeezed. Even though they may benefit from outsourcing some of their production to backstreet sweatshops, large corporations have an interest in regulating them when their use leads to this sort of cheap competition. In order to survive, they therefore have to protect their intellectual property and seek constantly to develop new, more complex products that cannot be easily imitated and can be sold on the basis that they are of high quality. In order to do so, they need skilled and creative workers who can not only help them innovate but will also be loyal to their employers. This in turn produces another contradiction: though on the one hand seeking to discipline their highly skilled and creative workers, extract their intellectual property, simplify their labor processes, and standardize them in the interests of "knowledge management" and "quality management," corporations also need to keep their skilled, creative workers motivated and encourage a flow of new ideas and a high quality of work. This gives some knowledge workers and skilled craft workers access to privileged positions in the labor market, with some bargaining power, even as others are being ousted from such positions.

These, then, are some of the contradictory features of the new landscape in which labor confronts capital in the twenty-first century. I hope that the essays in this collection will not only contribute to better understandings of this relationship but also point to some of the ways that labor can improve its ability to navigate it and identify new routes toward alternative destinations.

1. What Will We Do?

The Destruction of Occupational Identities in the Knowledge-Based Economy

Faced with the difficulty of placing a stranger, the most common opening gambit is to ask, "What do you do?" Except perhaps in a few small hunter-gatherer tribes, a person's occupation is one of the most important delineators of social identity. In many European cultures this is reflected in family names. People called Schmidt, Smith, Herrero, or Lefebvre, for instance, had ancestors who were iron workers. Wainwrights and Wagners are descended from wagon makers, and so on with the Mullers (millers), Boulangers (bakers), Guerreros (soldiers), and all the myriad Potters, Butchers, Carters, Coopers, Carpenters, Fishers, Shepherds, and Cooks whose names can be found in any North American phone book.

The phenomenon is by no means unique to cultures of European origin. In South Asia the division of labor evolved to become so embedded in other social structures that occupational identity was something you were born into. In the words of Sudheer Birodkar, "Occupational specialisation was the essence of the sub-division of the two lower Varnas (castes) of the Vaishyas and Shudras into the various Jatis (occupational sub-castes). . . . Infringement of caste rules of vocation could lead to expulsion; thus a Chamar (shoemaker) had to remain a Chamar all his life. If he tried to become a Kumar (potter) or Darji (tailor) he was in danger of being expelled from the Chamar caste and obviously under the caste rules he would not be admitted into any other caste in spite of his having the knowledge of any other vocation."[1]

Such discrete craft-based *occupational* identities began to break down under the impact of automation and the introduction of the factory system. Inherent in capitalist relations of production, according to Marxian theory, is the general tendency to reduce workers to an undifferentiated mass, who can easily replace each other—a working class or proletariat. There is a direct relationship between the degree of skill required to perform any given task and the scarcity of that skill and the ability of the workers who possess it to negotiate with employers (or, in the case of the self-employed, with customers) for high wages and decent working conditions. It is thus in the interests of capital to have a working class whose skills are as generic and substitutable as possible. Workers who have only generic skills are cheap to employ and can be gotten rid of if they become troublesome because substitutes can easily be found.

For socialists, occupational identity, constructed as it generally is around the possession of particular skills, knowledge, or experience, thus presents something of a conundrum. On the one hand, it forms a basic organizational building block; on the other it is a barrier to the development of broader class consciousness. Traditionally most (though not all) organizations of workers have grown up around specific occupational identities in groupings that are simultaneously inclusive, in the sense that they generate strong internal solidarities, and exclusive in the sense that they rely for their effectiveness on strong boundaries and restrictions on entry to the group.

Some of the mechanisms for limiting entry to the occupation, such as apprenticeships, can be traced back to precapitalist forms of organization, such as guilds, whose members were often obliged to take oaths to preserve the secrets of the trade in elaborate initiation rituals and to engage in other practices that consolidated the bonds between members but excluded outsiders. Even much newer occupation-based groupings often exhibit strong social homogeneity in their membership, giving a gendered and ethnic character to who is admitted and who excluded. This can make them divisive in relation to working people as a larger class.

However, through their strong organization and ability to resist being pushed around by the employers, such groups may play a progressive role in winning higher wages or improved conditions for some segments of the workforce or, more broadly, they may lead campaigns for protective legislation or welfare provisions that benefit the population in general. This has especially been the case in countries such as Germany, where social-democratic political parties have taken the lead in developing sector-based, rather than occupation-based, collective bargaining.

Although the welfare states that developed during the post–Second World War period in advanced capitalist countries took distinctive forms, all of them undoubtedly owe many of their achievements to the efforts of workers' organizations that were strong enough to compel employers to share some of the productivity gains of mass production. As a result, employers and states agreed to a kind of compromise in which they lessened their antagonism to workers' organizations and labor allowed employers to manage workplaces without constant threat of disruption.[2] Workers' organizations did differ in different countries; they were either explicitly occupation-based, as in the craft-based trade unions that were prevalent in the United Kingdom, or based in more general trade unions led by labor elites with strong occupational identities.[3] But it should be noted that this same period was also characterized by labor markets that were strongly segmented by gender and ethnicity, as well as being fractured along many other dimensions.

Skill does not just have a double-edged character for labor; it has an equally ambiguous meaning for capital. The innovation process that forms the necessary motor of change for capitalist development is deeply contradictory in its need for skill. Before a task can be automated, it is necessary to draw on the expertise and experience of someone who knows exactly how to do it: to anatomize every step in the process and work out how it can be standardized and how a machine can be programmed to repeat these steps. Once expropriated, the knowledge and experience—or "craft"—of these workers can be dispensed with, and cheaper, less-skilled workers can be substituted to operate the new machines.

But the need for skills does not stop there. Human knowledge, ingenuity, and creativity are also absolutely essential to invent and design new products and processes, customize them for new purposes, communicate and provide content for a wide range of products and services that keep the wheels of capitalism turning, and care for, educate, inform, distract, and entertain the population. Some of these functions are themselves subjected to processes whereby the knowledge of the workers is expropriated and incorporated into computer programs or databases so that the tasks can be carried out by fewer, or less-skilled, workers. Here, for instance, we could include the knowledge of specialists working on technical-support help desks who are encouraged to put the answers to frequently asked questions onto databases that can be accessed by more junior front-line staff, or the knowledge of university professors who are asked to convert their lectures into content for "e-learning" courses. But as one task becomes routinized and de-skilled, a new cohort of "knowledge workers" is required to devise the next stage in the commodification process.[4]

Arguments about whether the development of an ever more technologically complex capitalism results in de-skilling or re-skilling are therefore beside the point. The nature of innovation is such that both processes happen simultaneously: each new development in the technical division of labor entails a new split between "head" and "hands." In order to routinize the jobs of one group of workers, another generally smaller group with some sort of overview of the process is necessary. As workers resist or adapt to change and organize to protect their interests, new occupations are continuously being formed and older ones re-formed. Just as occupational identities can be said to be both exclusionary and inclusive, they can also be said to be in a continuous process of construction and deconstruction. Employers have to balance their interest in cheapening the value of labor with their need to ensure that there is a renewable supply of well-educated and creative workers with fresh new ideas. In some situations, companies also want to retain proprietary control over skills and knowledge that give them a competitive edge over their rivals.

It can be argued that traditional Marxian theory underestimates the importance of skill in shaping the ways in which labor markets function. The reality that has evolved is considerably more complex than the classic picture of a polarization of society between a bourgeoisie—that owns the means of production, controls the circulation of goods and capital, and dictates the functioning of the state—and an ever-more homogenous proletarian mass, whose members can be kept in line by the knowledge that any worker who demands too much can be replaced by someone else from the "reserve army" of the unemployed who can do the same work more cheaply or more compliantly. On the contrary, the evolution of an increasingly complex technical division of labor has created a constantly changing demand for an extremely diverse range of skills, many of which are specific to particular stages of industrial development, particular sectors, proprietary processes, products, or even specific companies.

However, despite this multiplication of tasks in a division of labor that is increasingly dispersed both contractually and geographically, the concept of the reserve army is still a relevant one that helps us make sense of many recent developments in labor markets, in this era in which the Post–World War II labor-employer-state compromise (sometimes described as the "Fordist deal") has either collapsed or is under severe strain. But in order to tease out these understandings, we need a more differentiated idea of the role played by occupational identities and skill in the functioning of labor markets. We also need to look more closely at the role played by the state in providing generic skills to a workforce that is required to fill niches in an increasingly complex and turbulent economy and at the role these generic skills play in eroding occupational boundaries and undermining the power of organized labor.

A starting point for this analysis is the idea of a labor market itself. There are of course many ways in which the very concept of a market in labor is questionable. There is an extreme asymmetry between the characteristics of labor and those of capital, which make the trade in labor quite different from trade in other goods and services. The human body, the basic unit offered on a labor market, has finite limits in terms of its strength, endurance, and agility, as well as in the number of consecutive hours it can keep going, which are different in character from the employing company's resources, which can be stretched as far as the limits of its access to capital and raw materials. Labor is not physically mobile in the way that capital is, and, in this era of free trade, when capital can cross national borders at will, labor is strongly constrained in its ability to tap into opportunities in other countries. It is often easier for your body parts to cross a national frontier after you are dead than it is for you as a living person to enter that country legally to seek work.

Labor markets are also distorted by many other factors, including monopolies and monopsonies (a single buyer of labor power), cartels, various forms of alliance among businesses or labor, state intervention, and other constraints on the availability of time or mobility (such as the need to carry out unpaid reproductive work) that reinforce gendered and racial divisions in the workforce. A market in which certain jobs are only available to men, or to white people, or to people of a certain religion, cannot by any means be characterized as a "free" market. The most important factor of all, however, in limiting access to jobs and preventing the development of "pure" competition in the market may be employers' needs for workers with specific skills in a highly complex—and increasingly global—technical division of labor.

One of the most important attempts to re-theorize labor markets was Peter Doeringer and Michael Piore's groundbreaking book, *Internal Labor Markets and Manpower Analysis*,[5] in which they developed the idea of *dual* labor markets. In this model, jobs fall roughly into two categories: those in "primary" or "internal" labor markets and those in "secondary" or "external" labor markets. Internal labor markets, they argued, are insulated from external market forces by internal rule systems. Employers who need particular skills, tuned to their own specific working practices, are prepared to offer inducements to keep loyal workers, including higher wages, pensions, holidays, and a range of other fringe benefits. Internal markets, they went on to say, are typically highly structured and hierarchical, with internal advancement paths, relying heavily on firm-specific knowledge. In these internal markets, employers are prepared to invest substantially in in-company training in order to achieve high levels of productivity. In other words, the levels of wages and conditions are different from those that would pertain in a "pure" external market. Entry points into these internal labor markets are hard to squeeze through, but once inside workers enjoy a number of benefits. In secondary or external labor markets the unspoken deal between capital and labor is very different: employers do not make a long-term commitment to the workforce but are prepared to accept lower levels of commitment and productivity from workers they feel free to lay off at will. Typical workers in internal labor markets at the end of the 1960s, when Doeringer and Piore were writing, would have been civil servants or employees of large companies such as IBM or General Motors; typical workers in external labor markets would have been janitors or waiters, or self-employed people who offered their skills to a range of different customers.

It soon became clear that this dual model was too simple to explain the complexity of wage differentials across whole diverse economies. Doeringer and Piore's insights were elaborated by other analysts, to develop models of multiple or *segmented* labor markets.[6] The concept of segmented labor markets recognizes that there may be numerous different labor markets in which wages and conditions are shaped by an interplay of factors including national education systems, industrial structures, cultural traditions, labor protection legislation, and the ways in which workers are organized.

In retrospect, we can see that the internal labor markets described by Doeringer and Piore and their followers were not absolute and unchanging features of the economic landscape. Rather, we may perceive them as specific to a certain phase of capitalism, namely, the period of postwar compromise. Although the death of this period is often proclaimed, we cannot be certain that elements of it will not continue to be useful or even necessary for capitalism in the future. However, it is reasonable to conclude that it is past its heyday. To understand how and why it has collapsed it is perhaps useful to look in a little more detail at how it functioned in its golden era.

First, it is necessary to emphasize that the special deal struck by capital with its essential "core" workers inside large organizations only functioned effectively because it did *not* cover all workers. Although there were historical moments when labor aristocracies used their power to win broad gains for much larger portions of the working class, the lucky insiders were kept aware of their privileged status and, on the whole, kept in order by the knowledge that life out there in the secondary labor market could be harsh. Patterns of inclusion and exclusion were often reinforced by ethnic and gender differences. Second, it is important to remember that the postwar model was not universal, but took different forms in different countries, shaped by their particular industrial structures and histories, including the specific ways that workers' organizations had evolved. In Germany, for instance, a strong social-democratic movement pushed for sector-level collective bargaining agreements, which meant that the "insider deal" was extended to all workers in a particular sector, rather than just to certain occupational groups (as was common where craft-based unions were strong, for instance in Britain) or in certain companies (as was the case where company-level bargaining was dominant). David Coates has provided us with an extensive analysis of the economy-wide implications of such differences, which have produced distinctive types of welfare systems, patterns of investment, degrees and types of government intervention, and particular training and qualification systems, which are in turn reflected in the ways occupations are defined.[7] Various types of "insider deal" are also complemented by specific types of "outsider deal," and this in turn means that the collapse of the postwar compromise took a unique form in each country.

In order to try to model some of these differences, I use a diagram adapted from Rosemary Crompton (see below) to integrate dual labor market theory with gender and class theory.[8] I have found this diagram useful for analyzing the differences between labor markets in different countries, and particularly for examining how they change in times of rapid structural and technological change, such as the one we are living through right now. This diagram takes internal and external labor markets as two extremes, shown here on the right and the left of the diagram (allowing for the possibility that there may be other intermediate types of labor

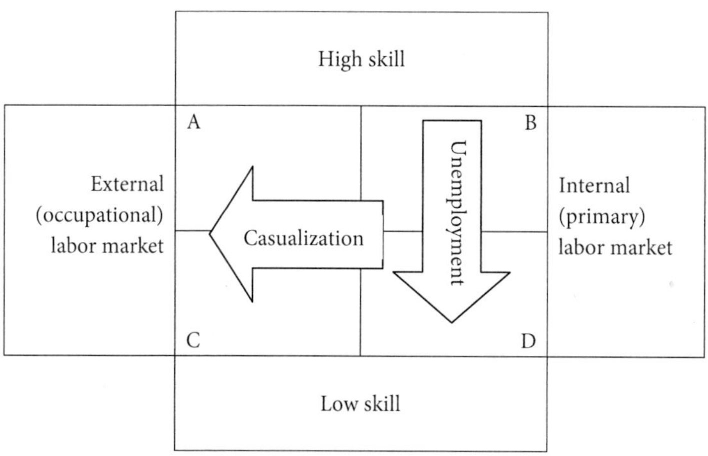

The structure of a labor market and the dynamics of restructuring

market segments placed somewhere between these extremes). It then adds another dimension, that of skill, shown here on the top and bottom of the diagram. It should in principle be possible to plot any kind of paid work somewhere in relation to these two axes. For instance, a highly paid executive of a large company or a senior civil servant would be somewhere near the top on the right-hand side, near corner B. But a highly paid freelance accountant working for a number of different clients, although still near the top in terms of skill level, would be over to the left near corner A. Down at the bottom on the right-hand side, near corner D, would be a new recruit or an apprentice at the bottom of the occupational ladder in a large stable institution (for example, a trainee mail sorter). Over on the bottom left, near corner C, would be a seasonal fruit-picker or a part-time, temporary burger-flipper. Again, there are many intermediate skill positions.

In a country like Germany, with its corporatist politics, historically strong internal labor markets, considerable employer investment in training and tightly defined occupational demarcations, and a welfare system closely linked to employer-based plans, we would expect a high proportion of the working population to be grouped toward the right-hand side of this diagram. A typical career trajectory would be to start down in corner D and work one's way up toward B, by taking the training courses provided by the employer and following the internal company rules.

In a more "liberal" labor market, such as that of the United States or the United Kingdom, the characteristic pattern would place a much higher proportion of the working population over on the left-hand side of the diagram—working contingently as self-employed individuals, or as temporary or part-time workers with little long-term job security and few chances for promotion within the firm or training beyond the immediate requirements of their job. Typically, the qualifications that workers do hold, beyond basic high school certification, have been acquired at their own expense or that of their parents. These labor markets could be expected to exhibit a stronger polarization, with major differences in living standards between a large undifferentiated mass of precarious workers near the C corner and the privileged few near A or B and considerable variation in between.

These are not, of course, the only two possible models. For example, we might expect the Scandinavian countries, with their strong welfare systems linked more to citizenship than to employment status and their commitment to publicly provided education and training, to have highly skilled working populations much more skewed to the top half of the diagram, with relatively few in either C or D. Many developing countries, in contrast, would be likely to have a very small formal sector, meaning that the great mass of the population is over on the left-hand side of the diagram in A or C.

Despite fairness rules, in all these types of labor markets, opportunities are not in practice available equally to the entire population. Lifelong resident (and white) men usually dominate the B quadrant of the diagram, with immigrants, people of color, and women more likely to be found down in the C quadrant.

This diagram is not just useful as a way of comparing static labor markets. It also helps us understand the different dynamic ways in which organizational restructuring affects workers in different national contexts. The employers' incentives to reduce the cost of labor may be the same wherever they are based, but in a "corporatist" labor market, where employees are protected by strong union agreements at a company or sector level, the boundaries of the internal labor market are firmly defined: either you are in or you are out. Just as the most usual way in is through formalized appointment procedures, so too the way out is likely to be through a formalized redundancy process. Workers who are inside the internal labor market have a lot to lose, since most of their welfare benefits are linked to their employment status, so they will fiercely resist expulsion and will often accept a radical restructuring of their work (for example, through accepting a breakdown of traditional job demarcations known as "multi-skilling" or a cut in take-home pay) rather than lose their toehold inside. Once unemployed, they find it difficult to find another job, partly because their skills may be very industry-specific or employer-specific and partly because employers are reluctant to create new jobs for people to whom they will have to make a long-term commitment. The route out of secure well-paid work is thus likely to follow the direction of the arrow I have marked "Unemployment" in the diagram.

In a less regulated labor market such as the United States and United Kingdom, internal labor markets are much less well-protected, and the benefits of being inside them are often relatively less. Here, employers are much more likely to respond to changing circumstances by "casualizing" employment. Increasing numbers of temporary workers are taken on to replace or supplement the work of full-time employees; staff with skills that are still required but not regularly are encouraged to go part-time or freelance; and increasing use is made of outsourcing. The way out of the internal labor market is thus more likely to follow the direction of the arrow I have labeled "Casualization" in the diagram. Although unemployment still exists in these countries (just as casualization takes place in countries like France, Germany, Austria, and Belgium) it is less likely to be absolute or of long duration. Instead, what can be seen is a general worsening of working conditions and growing insecurity, as a creeping precariousness spreads across the labor market like rust eating away at the old Fordist machinery.[9]

Do these differences matter? Readers of the business press will no doubt be used to finger-pointing articles blaming the five million unemployed in Germany on the "sclerotic" or "rigid" European labor market policies, just as readers of more liberal European journals will be familiar with stories about the overworked workers of the "Anglo-Saxon" countries who have given away their rights in a collective act of self-exploitation. Such perceptions do little to foster a sense of unity among workers. But traditional Marxists might argue that the great mass of the unemployed and the great mass of contingent workers nevertheless serve more or less the same function: they are the reserve army whose existence acts as a brake on workers' movements to improve pay and conditions in the more organized segments of the labor market.

There is only one problem with this approach. Modern economies now produce such a huge array of goods and services, involving such a wide range of different inputs in such complex configurations that for many tasks (though not all) simple muscle power is no longer enough. In other words, the technical division of labor has evolved to a point where most jobs actually require specific skills and a reserve army is no use unless it possesses them. These are not, however, in most cases the same skills that were required a generation ago—those skills around which the occupational identities of the second half of the twentieth century evolved. The jobs of the lathe turner, the linotype operator, the pattern cutter, the graphic designer, the film editor, the proofreader, the keypunch operator, the audio typist, the switchboard operator have all either gone the way of the handloom weaver or the scribe or been transformed out of all recognition. A key role in this transformation has been played by information technology. The use of computers has not ironed out the many differences that remain between different production processes, industries, and companies. However, it has introduced a range of standard processes for organizing and manipulating the information pertaining to them.

The proportion of the workforce that actually uses a computer in the course of its daily work varies from country to country but it is high and growing. And employers do not want to have to bargain with a small elite group of workers who understand how these computers work and are able to operate them (as some of them had to in the 1960s when computer programming was the exclusive—and mystifying—preserve of a few relatively privileged techies). Nor do they want to invest heavily in training them. What they need is a plentiful supply of computer-literate workers who can be taken on when they are needed and dropped when they are no longer required, with no fear of being left stranded without the necessary skills when demand picks up again. But how can they guarantee such a supply?

There is an interesting parallel here with what happened in the nineteenth century when the organization of industry and of national economies and empires became complex enough to require a workforce that was numerate and literate. Not only was an army of clerks necessary to process the invoices and receipts for all the transactions involved in international trade, there was also an increasing need for records to be kept of the work itself to note who had worked what hours and calculate their earnings. It was also useful even for manual workers to be able to read, write, and do simple arithmetic so that they could follow instructions, keep track of stock, and so on. If only a few people had these skills, that would have given them some bargaining power that would have restricted the employers' scope for maneuver. It was also, of course, necessary to ensure that new recruits arrived at the workplace already instilled with the values of punctuality, hard work, and respect for other people's property. Literacy and numeracy were also useful to people in their capacities as consumers—so that they could handle cash in an economy that increasingly relied on money, read public signs, and identify which goods to buy. What was the solution? Universal primary school education, teaching the "three R's" in an atmosphere in which authority was to be respected, a strong work ethic encouraged, and truancy or lapses in punctuality punished severely. Once these skills were universal, nobody could exert extra leverage in the market by possessing them.

Nowadays, both the rhetoric and the skills are a little different. Employers want people who are "digitally literate," "self-motivated," "good team players," and possess "soft skills," "employability," and "entrepreneurship." They also require people who are prepared to keep on learning new skills as the technology or the market changes, sometimes described as "a commitment to lifelong learning." And they need people who are familiar with or able to master a range of specific software packages and who can communicate with distant customers in a global market. Needless to say, these "skills," "competences," "aptitudes," and "know-how," combined in whatever pick-and-mix permutations, do not add up to stable occupational identities. In fact, they imply a world in which there are no limits, in the sense of "this is what I do, but this is what I don't do as part of my job," where each job description is infinitely elastic and there is never a point at which the worker can sit back and think, "At last, I'm trained. I have a recognized occupation. Now I can relax and just get on with the job." There is convincing evidence that we have now entered a phase of global capitalism in which, just like the need for universal literacy in the nineteenth century, there is now a universal need for new generic attitudes and abilities. And, just as in the nineteenth century, state agencies have leaped to the assistance of the employers to provide them. Only this time it isn't within national borders, or competing empires, but on a global scale.

It is never easy to disentangle capitalism's need to expand to find new markets from its need to tap into new sources of labor. Indeed, the two are intimately interconnected. However, it is hard to deny that the current educational policies of supranational bodies like the World Bank and the European Union, as well as those of the individual nations that are recipients of their aid, have, if not as an explicit aim, at least the effect of creating a global reserve army of "knowledge workers." In the process, any market advantages held by those who previously had more or less exclusive access to this knowledge are destroyed.

At a national level, these attempts take different forms in different developed countries. For instance in Austria, in keeping with the corporatist model, the government has set up *Arbeitsstiftungen*, labor foundations, which provide training for unemployed people in close cooperation with local employers. In one study by Hans Georg Zilian, in the district of Leoben, it was found that 38 percent of the trainees ended their spell of unemployment by returning to their former employers. Zilian concluded that these foundations act as holding tanks for the employers, where workers can be retrained at the taxpayer's expense until they are needed again.[10] In relation to our diagram, such activity can be seen as taking place near the D corner, with the state colluding with employers to co-regulate entry to what, though heavily eroded, could still be regarded as an internal labor market. In less regulated economies, training may be more likely to be carried out at the expense and initiative of the individual, and it can be conceptualized as taking place over on the left-hand side of the diagram, among the casualized workers who make up the A–C axis. In some cases the subsidy from the state to the employer may be less direct than simply paying for the training. Regardless of the precise role of the state, there is in general more and more emphasis in job advertisements as well as in training courses on the need for "e-skills" and "digital literacy." Across the European Union, the European Computer Driving License (ECDL) certifies that its owner has acquired basic computer skills.

At an international level, aid to developing countries for education is increasingly explicitly related to the development of a global "knowledge-based economy." The World Bank, for instance, links its aid closely to what it calls K4D, "knowledge for development," in programs that link educational reform with the extension of telecommunications networks, encouraging entrepreneurship, and "an efficient innovation system of firms, research centers, universities (and) consultants."[11] The aid programs of the European Union have similar objectives, for instance the EU's 2001 policy statement *Strengthening Cooperation with Third Countries*[12] states that the aim of its education policy is "to improve human resources management and to make the EU a powerful actor in education, training and R&D in a competitive world economy."[13]

Such programs often explicitly demand a dismantling of national qualification systems and links to international courses and curricula, including the franchising of courses run by universities and colleges in donor countries, the compulsory teaching of English in primary schools, and sometimes, a second European language in secondary schools, as well as the now familiar emphasis on "e-skills," "digital literacy," "employability," and "entrepreneurship." Multinational companies are also active in establishing global skill standards, for instance by providing certification courses in the use of proprietary software, like Microsoft's or SAP's, or donating hardware or telecommunications to schools and colleges to familiarize students with their products.

In the EU, under a series of "eEurope Action Plans," various targets for achieving general levels of computer science attainment, alongside other "knowledge society" indicators, such as levels of Internet access and usage of e-commerce, were set for the ten new member states that joined the EU in 2005, as well as for Romania, Bulgaria,[14] and Turkey, which are still waiting in the queue to join. The new member states in Central and Eastern Europe, including Hungary, the Czech Republic, Poland, Slovenia, Slovakia, Lithuania, Latvia, and Estonia, are already taking on the role of a cheap back office for the rest of the EU.[15] The "third countries" referred to in this policy document constitute an outer ring of countries beyond these: Albania, Bosnia and Herzegovina, Croatia, the Federal Republic of Yugoslavia, the former Yugoslav Republic of Macedonia, Armenia, Azerbaijan, Belarus, Georgia, Kazakhstan, Kyrgyzstan, Moldova, the Russian Federation, Tajikistan, Turkmenistan, Ukraine, Uzbekistan, Mongolia, Algeria, Egypt, Israel, Jordan, Lebanon. Morocco, Syria, Tunisia, and Palestine.

As these programs are rolled out, the populations of these countries can increasingly be set alongside those of established offshoring destinations such as India, the Philippines, or Barbados for the English-speaking world; Tunisia, Morocco, or Martinique for French speakers; or the Dominican Republic, Mexico, or Colombia for Spanish-speakers in the global race to the bottom for information workers. With high-capacity telecommunications infrastructure in place, and workers who speak the global languages and can use the increasingly standard global software packages, it will be possible to switch work seamlessly from worker to worker and place to place in the process increasingly known as "global sourcing"—a complicated mixing and matching of tasks from a number of different locations in specific configurations to suit a particular business client.

It is often assumed by workers in the developed economies that the point of moving work offshore is to eliminate the jobs back home. But this is to miss the point. The purpose of a reserve army is not to take over all the work but to act as a disciplinary force. The actual number of jobs being relocated overseas is tiny compared with the normal "churn" in national labor markets. National employers still need skilled workers in their home territory, near to where their clients are based, and most are reluctant to offshore their more sensitive "core" research and development work. In any case, many of the sectors in which offshoring is taking place, such as call centers, are still expanding. Companies also, of course, need a home market for their goods, something that would not exist if there were mass unemployment. The U.S. market is still many times larger than, for instance, that in China or India.

While not denying the real misery caused by the unemployment that is certainly taking place, it is nevertheless important to remember that the most powerful effect of offshoring is not to eliminate jobs in the United States or in Europe—it is to cheapen them. If workers know that the skills they have are also held by hundreds of thousands of other people around the world, then it is very difficult to organize on the basis of their unique occupational identities. And if they are aware that it would be perfectly feasible, technologically speaking, to move their jobs offshore, then this creates a potent disincentive to ask for improvements in wages and conditions or to refuse to take on extra tasks. Just the possibility that the job *might* move is enough to destroy workers' security and bargaining power. Although their employers still need creativity and knowledge and, often, highly specialized skills, these are less and less likely to be found within fixed and stable occupational identities.

In the destruction of these identities, are we witnessing the final death of the postwar high-wage, high-consumption deal and with it the end of job security? Or are we simply living through yet another twist in the development of capitalism? Will we see a collapse of organized labor into protectionism and racism, or will workers' ingenuity and ability to adapt and respond to new challenges lead to the development of new forms of organizing across national frontiers? And, when in the future people ask us, "What do you do?" what will we reply?

2. Fixed, Footloose, or Fractured

Work, Identity, and the Spatial Division of Labor in the Twenty-First-Century City

The combination of technological change and globalization is bringing about fundamental changes in who does what work where, when, and how. This has implications that are profoundly contradictory for the nature of jobs, for the people who carry them out, and hence for the nature of cities.

On one hand, work that previously was geographically tied to a particular place has become footloose to a historically unprecedented extent; on the other, there have been vast migrations of people crossing the planet in search of both jobs and personal safety. There has thus been a double uprooting—a movement of jobs to people and a movement of people to jobs. Between them, these upheavals are transforming the character of cities in both developed and developing countries.

In the process, they are also transforming social identities and structures. Most classic accounts of social stratification place a central importance on occupational identity. The basic building block of class identity has traditionally been the occupation, normally a stable identity acquired slowly either by inheritance or through a training process intended to equip the student or apprentice with skills for life. Once entered into this occupation and practicing those skills, the holder has a recognized position in the social division of labor that gives him or her a "place" in that society for life, barring some calamity such as illness, unemployment, or bankruptcy—risks against which the welfare states of most European countries provide some form of social insurance.

These identities have helped to give most cities a known shape that is familiar to their inhabitants: quarters that are homes to particular industries; recognized labor market institutions; characteristic family structures; and physical and social infrastructures that reflect and reinforce these patterns. Social structures and relationships are played out in the physical geography of the city: "male" spaces and "female" ones; "ghetto" areas where recently arrived immigrants are concentrated and areas where the indigenous inhabitants preponderate; noisy areas where young people congregate; and quiet ones where the elderly live. These patterns are shaped by gendered and racial patterns and structured by the power relationships between the different social groups. This does not just affect who lives where, who works where, or who chooses to travel where, but also how each area is subjectively experienced—for instance which areas are perceived by whom as clean, safe, or friendly.

The unprecedented movements of people and jobs around the world have coincided with a breakdown of many traditional occupational identities. Specific skills linked to the use of particular tools or machinery have increasingly given way to more generic and fast-changing skills linked to the use of information and communications technologies (for work involving the processing of information) or to new labor-saving technologies for manual work, for example in construction, manufacturing, packing, or cleaning. In many countries, this disintegration of occupational identities has also coincided with a collapse in the institutional forms of representation of workers, such as trade unions, which have in the past served to give some coherent shape and social visibility to these identities. We are left with a rapidly shifting and largely uncharted landscape in which jobs are created (and disappear) with great rapidity, often without even a concrete designation—just a pick-and-mix combination of "skills," "aptitudes," and "competences."

Without coherent and stable occupational identities as basic building blocks of social analysis, how can we begin to chart the changes currently taking place in our cities? One possibility is to start with their spatial rootedness. Here, a possible typology is to categorize them as "fixed" or "footloose," with an intermediate category for jobs that combine both fixed and footloose features that we might designate as "fractured."

One of the ironies of the present situation is that many of the most fixed jobs are often carried out by the most footloose people, while some of the most footloose jobs may be carried out by people with deep ancestral roots in the location in which they work.

Let us start with some of the fixed jobs. One of the most obvious characteristics of fixedness is the need for physical proximity to a particular spot, because the job directly involves the making, mending, cleaning, or moving of physical goods or the delivery of real personal services to people in real time and real space.

Starting with my own real space, I look around at the fixed jobs that sustain it. I live on a street of nineteenth-century three-story houses in London, of which around a third are occupied by single middle-class households, the remainder having been converted into apartments or occupied by larger, poorer extended families. Most of the middle-class households employ a cleaner for three or four hours a week. Of the cleaners I know on this street, one is Bolivian, one Mauritian, one Ugandan, and one Colombian. Not a single one is white; not a single one was born in Europe, let alone London. At the end of the road there are two restaurants, a café, a fish-and-chips shop, and a fried-chicken takeout outlet. One of the restaurants serves European-style dishes of various origins, mainly French. Its owner is a Montenegrin married to an Irish woman. The waitresses are Brazilian, Polish, and Russian.

The other restaurant advertises an Italian menu but is owned and staffed (with the exception of one Albanian waitress) by Turkish men, as is the café. The fish-and-chips shop is staffed by Chinese men. The fried-chicken outlet, which is open most of the night and caters to a rather rough clientele, is, despite its American name, staffed by a transient crew of exhausted-looking workers of African or Asian origins.

Periodically the houses on the street that are publicly owned (around 20 percent of the total) are renovated together. This happened last year, and for several weeks the neighborhood was filled with construction workers. This time, as far as we could tell, all the skilled workers were Polish; some of the less-skilled laborers were from various Balkan states. Apart from one surveyor (a black Londoner) I saw no women in the crew.

Not having a car, I make frequent use of a local minicab (cheap taxi) service. The drivers are constantly changing but include men from a large number of South Asian and African countries. To my knowledge there is only one woman driver, a feisty Nigerian who refuses to get out of her car but leans heavily on the horn to announce her arrival. I cannot remember the last time I was assigned a white driver.

This diversity of ethnic origin is not unique to manual work. The small company that maintains my computer network is run by a Greek Cypriot man. His deputy is Syrian and when he is too busy he sends a Turkish engineer to attend to my problem. All are highly skilled and educated. The reception desk at our local health center is staffed by two very efficient women—one Nigerian and one Somali.

Such examples could be multiplied many times, not just in London but in many cities across the globe where the maintenance of fixed infrastructure and customer-facing service activities are increasingly in the hands of people who were born in other countries or continents. Their presence as newcomers or temporary migrants has multiple effects on the shape and character of the host cities now dependent on their labor, both in the areas where they live and the areas where they work. As service workers and service users they are often at the interface of consumption and production in both public and private services and in the process both are transformed: markets are created for new kinds of food and personal services; health and educational institutions revise the hours and the languages in which services are available; and new codes of dress or behavior, tacit or explicit, are introduced, making multiple demands on both new and established residents whose social survival depends on learning how to decode them. The specific ethnic composition of any given city is shaped by a complex interplay of factors including its colonial history, political, religious, and cultural traditions, industrial structure, and geographical location; the fact of diversity, however, is increasingly universal.

So much for the fixed jobs—what of the footloose ones? The development of a global division of labor is not new. Regions have traded their goods with one another for as long as recorded history, and raiding other parts of the world for raw materials or slave labor is at least as old as colonialism. At the end of the nineteenth century the British Empire exhibited a remarkably developed pattern of regional industrial specialization knitted into a global trade network. The twentieth century saw multinational corporations operating with increasing independence of the interests of the nation-states in which they were based, ushering in a period after the Second World War that was characterized by Paul Baran and Paul Sweezy as "monopoly capitalism."[1] By the 1970s, it was clear that a "new global division of labor" was coming into being in manufacturing industry with companies breaking down their production processes into separate subprocesses and redistributing these activities around the globe to wherever conditions were most favorable.[2] These trends continued in the 1980s with industries as diverse as clothing, electronics, and auto manufacture dispersing their production facilities away from developed economies with high labor costs and strong environmental controls to developing countries, often in "free trade zones" where various tax incentives were offered and labor and environmental-protection regulations were suspended in an effort to attract as much foreign direct investment as possible. Workers in these zones were disproportionately young and female, and they received wages below subsistence level. Nevertheless, they were by no means passive and many actively organized to improve their lot.[3] This is one of the reasons why some of the regions once regarded as low-wage, for instance, Southeast Asia and Central America, are now seen as relatively high-wage, and companies have left them to exploit even cheaper workforces in places such as China, Sub-Saharan Africa, and other parts of Latin America.

Needless to say, this development had dramatic impacts on cities that lost manufacturing employment as well as those that gained it. In developing areas, such as the Mexican maquiladoras or the Philippines' Metro Manila region, huge new urban developments have sprung up, often highly polluted, whose economies depend on manufacturing for export. These areas attract labor from the impoverished rural peripheries and in the process create new urban markets for goods and services and new demands for infrastructure and housing that are frequently not met adequately.

In developed countries, cities that grew up as manufacturing centers in the nineteenth and early twentieth centuries had to transform into service centers or decline into collapsed rust-belt areas with high unemployment, empty shopping malls, rising crime, and deteriorating public services. In many cases they did not switch overnight from being employers of skilled, organized indigenous workers to wastelands of empty factories and warehouses. Instead they went through a transitional period during which the work was automated, simplified, and cheapened. Often an immigrant workforce was imported to carry out the jobs that were no longer attractive to indigenous people in the prosperous period that ran in most developed countries from the 1950s to the mid-1970s. When the factories began to close, from the mid-1970s on, it was these immigrant workers, whether South Asians in northern Britain, North Africans in France, Turks in Germany,

Hispanics in the United States, or Koreans in Japan, who bore the brunt of this development. Ethnic tensions were added to the brew of decline in the rust-belt areas.

Less well studied—at least until very recently—has been the new global division of labor in white-collar work. Nevertheless, this too has been progressing since the 1970s when low-skilled work such as data entry or typesetting began to be exported in bulk from North America and Europe to low-cost economies in the Caribbean, as well as South and Southeast Asia, while higher-skilled services, such as computer programming, started to be exported to the developed world from developing economies such as India, the Philippines, and Brazil.[4]

In 2000, the first research project aiming to map and measure the development of an international division of labor in telemediated information-processing work was launched under the acronym EMERGENCE (Estimation and Mapping of Employment Relocation in a Global Economy in the New Communications Environment). Under my direction, EMERGENCE was initially funded by the European Commission's Information Society Program to carry out research in the fifteen nations that were then full member states of the European Union plus the candidate states (now full members) of Hungary, Poland, and the Czech Republic. The project later attracted further funds to carry out related research in Australia, the Americas, and Asia. In the process it has built up a multifaceted picture of the complex and rapidly changing new global division of labor in information services. The first question asked was to what extent employers are actually using the new technologies to relocate work. A survey was carried out of 7,268 establishments with fifty or more employees in the eighteen European countries and a comparable survey of 1,031 establishments of all sizes in Australia. The survey looked systematically at the locations where seven different generic business services were carried out. These business services were: creative and content-generating activities, including research and development; software development; data entry and typing; management functions (including human resource management and training as well as logistics management); financial functions; sales activities; and customer service (including the provision of advice and information to the public as well as after-sales support). For each function, the survey looked at the extent to which it was carried out remotely using a telecommunications link—"eWork"—whether it was carried out in-house or outsourced, and the reasons for the choice of any particular location or outsourcer.

The results gave a comprehensive picture of the extent to which these business services were already delocalized in the year 2000. In Europe, nearly half of all establishments were already carrying out at least one function remotely using a telecommunications link to deliver the work, and around a quarter were doing so in Australia.

Even more striking than the overall extent of eWork is the form it takes. Most literature on "remote work," "telecommuting," "teleworking," or any of the other pseudonyms for eWork presupposes that the dominant form is home-based work. Yet these results show that the stereotypical "eWorker" based solely at home is in fact one of the least popular forms. Moreover, in-house eWorking is heavily outweighed by "eOutsourcing" as a mechanism for organizing work remotely, with some 43 percent of European employers and 26 percent of Australians making use of this practice. Much eOutsourcing is carried out within the region in which the employer is based (34.5 percent), but substantial numbers (18.3 percent) outsource to other regions within the same country, and 5.3 percent outsource outside their national borders. These interregional and international (sometimes inter-continental) relocations of work provide clues to the geography of the emerging international division of labor in "eServices."

What are the main factors propelling this move to outsource beyond national borders? At the top of the list is the quest for the right technical expertise. Only when this is available do secondary factors come into play such as reliability, reputation, and low cost. It is this factor more than anything that explains the importance of India in the supply of eServices. With its vast population India seems to offer an almost unlimited supply of English-speaking computer science graduates. A survey of 200 of the largest companies in the United Kingdom, commissioned in 2001 by a leading international outsourcer, found that India was the offshore software development center of choice for 47 percent of managers.[5] There are already signs, however, that the Indian software market is overheating, despite the drastic drop in demand from the United States since the bursting of the dot-com bubble. Some Indian companies have already moved into intermediary positions in the value chain and are outsourcing to other destinations including Russia, Bulgaria, Hungary, and the Philippines.[6]

For lower value-added activities like data entry cheaper countries, including Sri Lanka, Madagascar, and the Dominican Republic, have established themselves as alternative destinations to the earlier players (like Barbados and the Philippines). China is gaining ground with an even larger population and lower costs than India, as well as a determination to acquire a leading role in the "eEconomy."

Different business functions are characterized by different types of workers. Lower-skill functions like data entry or customer service work tend to involve large numbers of workers who are more likely to be women; higher-skilled functions like systems design generally employ smaller numbers, who are more likely to be male.

As companies find themselves with global options to choose from, they become ever more picky about where to go, choosing suppliers or locations on a "horses for courses" basis. In the process some regions (Bangalore in South India is a classic example) develop worldwide reputations for excellence in a particular field, while others are completely bypassed. Large sections of the world, including much of Sub-Saharan Africa and Central Asia, were classified by the EMERGENCE project as "e-Losers."[7]

What has happened since 2000? A second series of case studies, carried out by the Asian EMERGENCE project in 2002 and 2003,[8] found that there had been significant developments in the early years of the twenty-first century. What was still a risky experiment at the turn of the millennium had become normal, not to say routine, business practice three years later. Value chains were getting longer and more complex, with more and more intermediaries involved. The world was witnessing the emergence of huge new companies involved in the supply of business services, often many times bigger than their clients, with an internal global division of labor. When a large organization in the private or public sector decides to outsource a major contract to supply business services, it is increasingly not so much a case of choosing between India or Russia, Canada or China, but more a question of deciding on a particular company (for instance Accenture, EDS, or Siemens Business Services). Once that company has the contract, it may decide to divide up the work between teams in many parts of the world, depending on the particular balance of skills, languages, cost, and quality criteria involved. This type of work could be regarded in many ways as a paradigmatic case of footlooseness, sliding without friction between teams across the globe that are linked by telecommunications networks and a common corporate culture but may nevertheless be physically located in strongly contrasting environments, and occupying very different social locations in the local class structure.

The presence of this new international class of cyberworkers undoubtedly impacts the cities in which they live. For instance, they may become conduits for spreading the values and cultures of multinational corporations outward into their local communities and down the value chain into supplying companies. If they leave to work for other, locally based, companies or decide to start a business on their own, these too will bear the marks of the international experience. There are other, more concrete effects. For instance, the impact of the international software industry on Bangalore has been dramatic in terms of creating pressure on the infrastructure and increases in property prices that affect the other residents of the city regardless of whether they work in the industry or not. Inhabitants of other cities have also become victims of the international success of some of their neighbors—for example Dublin's (temporary) success as part of the Celtic Tiger phenomenon produced chronic traffic congestion and a property price inflation that put buying a home beyond the reach of many who could previously have afforded it. Once the bubble burst, many were left with unaffordable mortgages. Similarly, traffic comes to a standstill every time there is a shift change in the booming call-center sites of Noida and Gurgaon near Delhi in northern India.

Meanwhile, the very fact that their work could be relocated to another part of the world places a brake on the prospects for white-collar workers in the cities where such jobs have traditionally been based. The increased precariousness of their jobs, often expressed contractually as self-employment or a temporary contract, does not just make it harder for them to seek improvements in their pay and conditions, it may also impact the local housing market by making it impossible for them to get a mortgage.

So far I have drawn a strongly dichotomous picture of a world in which the fixed is counterposed to the footloose in relation both to jobs and to people. For many of us, of course, the reality is much more complex than that, exhibiting both fixed and footloose features in complex configurations. I have termed this condition "fractured." In a fractured existence, the characteristics of fixedness and footlooseness are in constant, tense interaction with each other. Rooted real-time activities (like putting the children to bed or eating a meal) are constantly interrupted by "virtual" ones (like the ringing of the telephone), while "virtual" activities (like checking one's e-mail) are disturbed by the physical realities of the situation in which one is placed (the pain of a stiff neck, for instance, or the impact of a power outage). The traditional diurnal rhythms of life are disrupted by requirements to respond to global demands. The interpenetration of time zones in one sphere of life leads inexorably to the development of a twenty-four-hour economy as people who are forced to work nontraditional hours then need to satisfy their needs as consumers during abnormal times, which in turn obliges another group to be on duty to provide these services, ratcheting up a process whereby opening hours are slowly extended right across the economy, and with them the expectation that it is normal for everything always to be open. This normalization process is accelerated by the existence in each city of growing numbers of new residents whose comparative frame of reference is spatial not temporal. Instead of comparing the opening hours of shops in a European city with how they used to be in the past, they are more likely to be comparing them with those in Nairobi, New York, or New Delhi. New immigrants are unlikely to be aware of the social solidarity that underpinned the reasons for many of the traditional time structures or, if they are, regard them as no more than quaint anomalies (or even racist practices designed to thwart them). For instance, from the 1950s to the 1980s in the United Kingdom, most shops in most towns were closed for half a day each week, known as "early closing day." Although this posed minor inconvenience to shoppers, it was almost universally accepted as fair, since shop assistants had to work on Saturday morning and therefore deserved a half-day off to compensate at another time during the week. Such attitudes are almost inconceivable in the twenty-first century.

This fractured experience of space and time is mirrored in the fracturing of occupational identities. Although many job descriptions retain a mix of fixed and footloose features, these are increasingly volatile. There has been an erosion of the clear boundaries of the workplace and the workday, with a spillover of many activities into the home or other locations, including an expectation that you should continue to be productive while traveling, whether you are a truck driver taking orders over a mobile phone during your lunch break or an executive working on a spreadsheet in an airport departure lounge. In a world in which the responsibilities for home and children are unevenly distributed between the sexes, these impacts are far from gender neutral and have contributed to an invisible redrawing of the boundaries between the jobs that can easily and safely be done by women and those that announce themselves subliminally as masculine.

Accompanying these dissolutions of the old unities of space and time, there has also been a redesign of many work processes involving some subtle and other not-so-subtle shifts in responsibility for particular tasks within most workplaces. Some of these changes have the cumulative effect of tipping the balance between fixedness and footlooseness. For example, a job that previously combined meeting and greeting customers with more backroom activities might become totally computer-based, making it easy to relocate it either wholly or in part to another location. If that other location is the existing worker's own home, then this might be experienced as quite liberating, but if the skills are not unique to the worker, the chances are the other location could be somebody else's desk on the other side of the world; far from being liberating this would then constitute a new source of precariousness. Conversely, some other tasks that were previously deskbound (and hence in principle delocalizable) may be redesigned to involve more customer-interfacing activities and become more spatially bound, although they may be tied not to a single location but multiple ones if the worker is expected to venture out to meet clients.

More invidious is the slow erosion of occupational boundaries and with it occupational identities. It is easy to caricature as rigid and hierarchical the old world in which everyone knew "this task is what I do; that task is what you do; that task is reserved for new young trainees; that one is only done by very experienced older workers who know what can go wrong." Apart from anything else, it could easily lead to a set of unspoken rules that assigned certain tasks to women or to members of particular ethnic groups or people with a particular educational background. This poses unacceptable barriers to social mobility and equality of opportunity. But without this, what do we have? A world in which you are always only as good as last week's performance; where to keep your job you must always be prepared to learn new skills and change the old ways you were trained in (and in which you may have taken pride in the past); where you cannot know reliably in advance when you will be free and when you will have to work; where you can never say "No, that is not my responsibility" without fear of reprisal. A world without occupational boundaries could very easily become a world in which social solidarity is well-nigh impossible because you no longer have any clear way of defining who your coworkers or your neighbors are, and one in which so many of your interactions are with strangers that it is hard to tell friend or ally from threat or enemy.

The future of our cities will depend in large part on how we reintegrate these fractured selves, workplaces, and neighborhoods.

3. Begging and Bragging

The Self and the Commodification of Intellectual Activity

There are always risks involved in giving a lecture like this.[1] There is a risk that, in assembling such a broad range of people from so many different parts of one's life one ends up, in the attempt to interest and please everyone, boring or annoying the entire audience. There are the twin risks of under- or overpreparing: the first leading to drying up; the latter to the woodenness of delivery that comes from remembering (or, worse, reading) words having almost forgotten the meaning they were originally intended to convey. And of course there is the general occupational risk that every writer, teacher, preacher and politician takes, of simply making a fool of oneself.

Being more of a fool than an angel, I have managed to add several further risks to these. I have chosen a title that, even allowing for the vogueishness of self-referentiality, offers a hostage to fortune. The very act of giving this lecture, of course, exposes me very directly to the risk of being accused of bragging, if not begging. More seriously, I have taken the much bigger risk of venturing into territory that, for me at least, is rather poorly charted. It would have been much safer to have picked a topic about which I have written and spoken many times before: a topic where every crack in the masonry is familiar and it is possible to predict which arguments will surprise and which will reinforce an audience's expectations and ensure that every assertion is suitably defended against the usual run of counter-arguments. But, as John Berger once said in a lecture I remember attending at the Institute of Contemporary Arts in London, some time in the 1970s, "The first time you say something, you're discovering a truth; the second time you say it, it's a little less true." So I have chosen instead to present something that is very much work in progress. It draws on a number of different strands in my work over the last thirty years or so, but these are so disparate that I am not at all sure they can be knitted together very coherently. I suspect that the fabric has some knots in it, as well as holes. But at least that gives you something to pick at, or stick your fingers through.

The strands that make it up come from my life as well as my reading. They include the experiences of trying to function with a reasonable degree of integrity and autonomy in most of the places intellectuals have earned their livings in Britain over the last forty years or so: in publishing, in television, in the voluntary sector, in quangos,[2] in local government, in universities and private research institutes, as an employee, as an employer, and as a freelance. The mental activity involved has carried a similarly disparate range of occupational designations: editor, writer, journalist, art historian, researcher, picture researcher, project officer, director, consultant, reviewer, evaluator, independent expert, manager, lecturer—and now professor. But across all these occupational groups and in all these settings I have seen similar developments, many of which sit in tension if not contradiction with each other: increasing intensification of work, standardization of processes, the introduction of performance indicators and targets, short-term contracts, project-based work, lengthening of working hours, and stress. During this same period there has been a great deal of rhetoric about removing the rigidities of the Fordist era and creating more individualized and flexible working conditions. We have been told by Richard

Florida that we are witnessing the rise of a "creative class,"[3] and by innumerable policymakers that we are entering a knowledge-based society in which we can all become "digital nomads"[4] or "symbolic analysts"[5] or even "portfolio men."[6] Yet everywhere I look what I see is more, not less bureaucratization, and less, not more autonomy.

The idea of slowly building a career and reputation on past achievements seems to be crumbling. Your credentials have to be proved anew every time you pass "Go." Whether you want to get a job or a pay raise or a research contract, whether you want to publish a book, obtain sponsorship for a film or funding for a conference, the first thing you have to do is fill in an application form. This involves an extraordinary act of mental contortion. First you have to understand the logic of the form designer, then you have to critically analyze your own nuanced and contradictory life and self and reduce its complexity to something that can be squeezed into the steely categories this logic has constructed. The more creative people are, the more interdisciplinary their methodology, the wider their knowledge, the more broad-ranging their experience, the less likely they are to fit the preconceptions of the bureaucrats and techno-nerds who designed the forms. A really original idea will, by definition, be something that nobody has yet thought of, so the chances of finding a ready-made category for it in a call for proposals is vanishingly unlikely. Similarly, if someone has made a really big theoretical breakthrough linking two previously quite disparate bodies of thought, then their chances of finding a home for it in a peer-reviewed journal will be much less than those of someone who is following a well-trodden track within a recognized discipline (or, these days, more probably a sub-sub-discipline). Even more frustrating is the position of someone who wants to do something exploratory—following a train of thought without being sure where it will lead. How can they possibly get started in a system in which you are increasingly required to specify in advance what it is that you will produce (usually broken down into "work packages" with specified "milestones," "deliverables," "outcomes," or "verifiable measures"). Trying to explain in advance why an innovation might emerge from a particular process is as tortuous and self-defeating as convincing a committee that an as yet untold joke might be funny.

How has this state of affairs come about? How is it that anyone who wants to receive any income whatsoever for doing something with their minds has to spend a working life jumping through these bureaucratic hoops? It is not just a question of the tedium and frustration of remembering innumerable passwords and pin numbers, retrieving innumerable reference numbers, keeping records of the time and place and duration and monetary value of every activity, however trivial, to be reentered repeatedly in ever-so-slightly different formats into those ubiquitous forms. Something much deeper and more damaging is taking place: we are being forced, over and over again, to go through a dual process that I have called begging and bragging. Even the lucky few in permanent jobs can't escape it. Look, for instance, at the Research Assessment Exercise currently going on in British universities. Even—or perhaps I should say especially—the most senior professors are regularly required to select their best publications (by whose standards?), list the conferences they have spoken at and the grants they have brought in, and brag about the "esteem" in which they are held.[7] Being told that this esteem is actually rather low is no doubt a minor humiliation compared with the psychic damage that results from being rejected outright for a job, or having one's research application turned down, but there is a cumulative battering of the ego that cannot be good for anyone's self-respect even for those who (by definition a minority) emerge from the process as winners most of the time. The harm doesn't just come from the inordinate amount of time that is wasted or the external rebuffs; for many people there is also pain, or at least discomfort, that arises from within: from the forced overriding of the ethical codes with which they were brought up. "Modesty is a virtue," "Don't show off," "Nice girls don't flaunt it," "Don't blow your own trumpet," "The empty vessel makes most noise," "The meek shall inherit the earth," or similar phrases told most of us in childhood that bragging is not what a well-brought-up person does. Similar injunctions, at least in countries with a Protestant tradition, tell us that begging is demeaning and bad for the character: "Stand on your own two feet," "Neither a borrower nor a lender be," "Don't spend what you haven't got," whereas "Beggars can't be choosers" makes it pretty clear that in entering a relationship with a funder or boss as a supplicant one is saying goodbye to any notion of a dialogue between equals.

It is my contention that the need to repeatedly take part in those peculiar rituals of boasting and supplication that are embodied in the processes of applying for jobs, grants, and commissions do violence to the personal values of those who subscribe, consciously or unconsciously, to ethical codes grounded in notions of honor, comradeship, self-respect, or the teachings of the great world religions. Responses from the morally sensitive range from a mild discomfort at having done something one's grandmother wouldn't have approved of to a strong sense of shame or disgrace tantamount to sin. But, I would argue, they also inflict terrible damage even on those who have no such scruples and lack even utilitarian ethical codes. And they do this by exposing just about everyone to repeated experiences of rejection. If we postulate, for the sake of argument, that twenty people on average apply for every job, of whom four are shortlisted, then nineteen of those people, having been forced to go through the process of saying how wonderful they are, are told "Well, actually no, you're not wonderful at all," and three have had to endure the ritualized humiliation of a job interview needlessly.

In the past, such repeated rejection was only experienced by a relatively small minority of the population (for instance, day laborers). Most people, at least most men, had continuous work that reinforced their sense of themselves and their own value, although of course this was not without its petty humiliations. Now that rejection is the dominant experience, we must ask ourselves what sort of a society it is producing. What kind of armor plating do we require to survive this repeated battering of our self-esteem? Are we producing people who cannot express vulnerability or empathy and never dare admit they are wrong? And what kinds of relationships can such people enjoy?

Reflecting on such work experiences and puzzling over their causes is, then, the first strand in this lecture. A second strand also derives from personal experience, but in this case it is my experience of unpaid work over the years as a campaigner and activist in trade unions, women's organizations, and community organizations. And it is here, ironically enough, that with hindsight we can see that some of the bars of this particular iron cage were forged.[8] I say "ironically" because, for many of the generation that came to adulthood in the 1960s, the strongest impulse behind the involvement in radical social movements was the desire for liberation from rigid and oppressive rule systems. It is of course dangerous to extrapolate too broadly from one's own experiences to those of an entire generation, and I would not wish to claim too much authority for my own memories. However, there was one institution of the 1970s—more or less unique to that period—that does give some justification for generalizing at least to a subset of that generation and that is the women's group. Of course, not all women defined themselves as feminists at the time, and not all of those who identified themselves as part of the women's liberation movement joined women's groups. Yet quite a few did, and because those who did were also those most likely to be actively involved in campaigns for equality of opportunity, women's groups deserve some special attention as sites for the exploration of the contradictions that arose between the conflicting desires for individual expression and for solidarity, for autonomy, and for fairness and, in a kind of dress rehearsal for the broader policy debates of the 1980s and 1990s, between the desires for security and stability on the one hand and adaptability and flexibility on the other.

Between 1972 and about 1987 (the last two faded out gradually so it was difficult to date their final demise) I was a member of several women's groups, in London and in Yorkshire, which spanned an often overlapping range including consciousness-raising groups, personal support groups, study groups, caucus groups, solidarity groups, and campaigning groups. None documented their work systematically, but enough of the members participated in the great outpourings of feminist writing of the period to make it possible to access their thoughts at the time without the distorting lens of individual hindsight. From these writings, and those of our contemporaries, it is clear that the name "Women's Liberation Movement" was adopted at least in part because it resonated so well with a dominant preoccupation as the 1970s dawned. This was a generation in full revolt against the staid social rigidities of the 1950s, when cloth-capped manual workers and their pinafored wives knew their place—below that of the bowler-hatted men and white-gloved ladies of the middle classes—when a child's place was in a uniform behind a school desk, a young man's place was in the army, and a woman's place was in the home. The image of the prison was frequently used to describe social institutions, including the family, as in Lee Comer's *Wedlocked Women.*[9] As Liz Heron pointed out,[10] these young women were the first products of the postwar welfare state with its free secondary education and low rates of unemployment, and had grown up witnessing the end of British colonialism. Their lives, compared with those of their parents, really did seem to be materially easier, and there was little reason for them to doubt that progress would continue to deliver plenty and inequalities would wither away (although the first encounter with the realities of the labor market often delivered a nasty shock to these expectations). Asked what they wanted, many would have replied simply "Freedom"—freedom to wear what they wanted, to have sex where, when, and with whom they wanted, and to express themselves how they wanted. Insofar as they shared these libertarian values, they can be seen as part of the same movement that gave us hippies, a movement that was anti-bureaucratic in the extreme. However, this was only part of the story. The first anthology of papers from the British women's movement, *Conditions of Illusion*,[11] whose title refers to

Marx,[12] had, by 1974, already dropped the word *liberation* from its subtitle and, along with the articles about "vaginal politics," psychiatry, sexuality, abortion, violence, child-rearing, marriage, the family, sex-role conditioning, and art, it had included a number of descriptions of campaigns, charters, and manifestos calling for equality in the workplace and an end to discrimination.

Here, manifest right from the infancy of its second wave, is an illustration of the central contradiction of feminism, that it tends to give rise to precisely those characteristics that it initially sprang up to oppose: the collapsing of half the human race into a single, undifferentiated category labeled "women." The impetus for liberation sprang, for many, from an insistence that each woman, as an autonomous subject, has as much right to express her own unique views, to shape her own destiny, and leave her own distinctive footprint on the world as any man. Underlying much early feminist writing one can detect a great yearning to speak for oneself, not as a representative of any abstraction of sex, race, or class, but simply as a unique and individual voice that will be listened to with respect. It is essentially the same dream as that expressed in his famous Washington speech by Martin Luther King for his four children, that they will be judged "not by the color of their skin but by the strength of their character." Yet in the search for the expression of this individuality, women came up, again and again, often at first with a terrible shock, against the hypocrisy of the ideas of democracy and equality they had been brought up to believe in, against forms of discrimination and stereotyping that were not just damaging economically but wounding to the psyche. The girl who had worked hard at school to excel in her exams and then found that it was her brother, with much poorer results, who was sent by the family to college; the student who thought her professor was interested in what she had written and discovered too late that he only wanted to get her into bed; the production-line worker who realized she would never be promoted to supervisor however hard she worked—all experienced the same reaction: it's so *unfair*. And, in struggling to make sense of this individual injury, at least some of these women were led to make generalizations: to see that they were prevented from fulfilling themselves in the way that they wanted *because* they were women (or, in some cases, *because* of their religion, class, ethnicity, color, disability, or some other variable). From this, it followed that they had a collective interest with others who shared the same characteristic, and from this realization, in turn, followed forms of organizing that were based on these shared identities. In this process, slowly but surely, the collective identity took precedence over the individual one. But not without a struggle. There was always a tension between the values of solidarity, cooperation, knowledge-sharing, and collective struggle and those of individualism, competition, and the desire for personal recognition, and attempting to resolve this tension presented huge challenges for individual behavior.

It is difficult to demand of anyone that she make personal sacrifices for a collective cause, and it seems likely that the limits of the appeal of feminism for many women can be found in this contradiction. A movement that bases itself intellectually on a rejection of the conventions that dictate how a woman should be a chaste daughter, a dutiful wife, a compliant worker, or a good mother must have something better to offer than an alternative set of "oughts"; it is not good enough to replace rule by patriarchy with rule by guilt-trip. This perhaps partly explains the demise of the women's movement *as* a "movement" explicitly aiming for personal liberation, although of course this demise must also be linked with the general defeat of working-class and other emancipatory movements during the Thatcher years.

What concerns me now is the legacy the women's movement left behind. To the extent that it was successful, the women's movement, along with other campaigns of the 1970s for justice and equality both within and without the labor movement, contributed to the development of a wide range of action plans, equal opportunity policies, and procedures designed to avoid discrimination, many of which are still extant. Like other regulations and formal rules of fairness, these procedures are a bit like the barbed wire and earthworks that mark the front line in trench warfare. While the war is actively being fought, they show how far one side has managed to advance and the extent to which the other has resisted, just as the labor legislation in a given state demarcates the state of play between capital and organized labor the last time they clashed. If the war is no longer actively being fought, however, these procedures may be experienced as an irritating hazard in the landscape, something that has to be stepped around and impedes personal progress. There are of course many workplaces, especially in the public sector, where the troops are still on the ground, in good spirits, still pushing the front line forward or actively resisting its pushing back. In others, though, it seems possible that these hard-won rules of fairness have become so embedded in the normal bureaucratic procedures that many people are not even sure why they are there beyond a general sense that "they are for your own protection" (rather like the passwords and pins we now have to remember to get access to just about any service whether it is the use of our own bank accounts or of our own computers or telephones). Bureaucratic rules are usually seen as taking their forms primarily from top-down pressures to rationalize processes and make them efficient. It is of course a commonplace of sociology that such pressures do not go unresisted and that institutions are shaped by the agency of those who inhabit and use them as well as by structural forces. But to my knowledge nobody has ever systematically studied the role of bottom-up pressure for rules of fairness in the formation of bureaucratic structures. I mention this now partly to avoid the accusation of adopting an overly structuralist approach in the next part of this lecture and partly to draw attention to the ways in which these structures do not take a single inevitable form but are capable of being reshaped in a variety of different ways if the political will is there to do so.

Having touched on the things I have observed in my employment history and through my involvement in various campaigns, I would now like to move on to some of the actual research and writing I have done. This too is rather diverse and does not follow a simple trajectory. It can be grouped very broadly into three categories: first, theoretical work mostly undertaken as a spare time activity outside the scope of any academic employment or research funding; second, empirical research, mostly focused in some way on the restructuring of work and carried out within the framework of formal research and consultancy contracts; and finally, more reflexive work on research methods, ethics, and practice, some of it developed through my teaching here at this university[13] during the early 1990s and some more recently through the RESPECT project[14] and participation in various evaluation and ethical panels. These activities have cross-fertilized each other, but I cannot claim to have linked them into a single coherent whole. Nevertheless, each has yielded some insights into my topic, so I am going to try now to make a first stab at bringing them together.

First, the theoretical work. One of the most important concepts in the development of my thinking has been that of commodification as an engine of economic, technological, and (in consequence of these) social change. By commodification I mean the tendency in capitalist economies to transform ever more activities into products or services that can be delivered in multiple standardized versions, thus enabling profits to grow in proportion to the volume of sales. The search for new activities to commodify is not the only driver of capitalist expansion. It is interlinked in complex ways with the need for expansion for other purposes: to find new markets, to find new sources of cheap labor, to find new sites of capital accumulation, and to find sites for the exploitation of natural resources as well as places to dump the waste resulting from all this destructive economic activity. I will concentrate here, though, on the commodification imperative. This expansion does not only take the form of spatial extension into relatively underdeveloped parts of the world (although this is nevertheless important), it also entails the extension of market relations into areas of life that have previously been outside the market. This can be conceived as a transformation of use values into exchange values. When I first started thinking about this, sometime in the late 1970s,[15] the sort of use values I mainly had in mind were those produced by unpaid labor in the home. This sort of commodification is still important. For evidence of this one only has to look at the continuing growth of the markets for convenience foods, domestic appliances, or do-it-yourself products. However, in the current neoliberal phase of capitalist expansion, another form of use value has also become a very attractive field for the development of new commodities. This is the public sector, where a range of activities, including education, health, and social care, are currently being commodified.

Although it is often associated with privatization, this form of commodification does not necessarily involve a change of formal ownership. It nevertheless brings about enormous changes in the nature of the work, in how work is managed, and in the relationship between workers and the users of their services (increasingly likely to be referred to as "customers"). Using principles of "scientific management" fundamentally unaltered since they were developed in the nineteenth century by the likes of Babbage and Taylor, work processes are analyzed and broken down into standardized units. Once these standardized units have been defined, performance indicators can be identified and standard protocols or quality control procedures introduced. These standardization processes make it possible to use information and communication technologies more extensively, for instance by introducing standard reporting procedures that make it possible to compare performance over time or between different locations, by making it possible to pool knowledge in common databases or "knowledge banks," and by making it possible to overcome the limits of space and time. In a mutually reinforcing process, the use of these technologies encourages further standardization, which in turn makes more intensive use of the technology possible. With each stage in this development, the nature of the activities becomes more generic.

Once processes have been standardized, or "modularized," it becomes possible for the units to be reconfigured in different permutations and combinations. They can be decentralized to scattered locations or they can be concentrated into centralized ones. They can continue to be carried out in-house or they can be outsourced or delivered through some partnership arrangement. Administrative tasks that used to be carried out in one central department may be broken up into small separate sub-tasks, each with its own targets, each of which could be the subject of a separate specification and a separate call for tender. Each of these could be carried out by a separate entity, but it could be (and increasingly is) the same giant multinational company that ends up winning the majority of these contracts, which can then be reintegrated in a new configuration, with the work spread across a global network of back offices. This explains the apparent paradox that both fragmentation and consolidation processes can be at work simultaneously.

This is not the place to try to map the full scope of this restructuring (although this is addressed in some of my past and current research). What I would like to concentrate on here is the impact on what might be called mental labor, or intellectual activity. At the simplest level, it can be postulated that if commodification is the engine, then intellectual labor is the spark that fires it. Without human ingenuity and cooperation none of the processes I have just described could take place. However, the story is much more complicated than that. Intellectual labor is not only crucially important for the further development of commodification, it is also itself subject to commodification processes and hence to the discipline of the market.

In order to understand what is happening to intellectual labor, it is necessary to take a broader look at the technical division of labor across the economy and the way in which it is constantly being restructured through the combined impact of technological change, standardization, and "scientific management" processes. This changing division of labor has to be understood as a contradictory phenomenon. The commodification process drives a continuous process of restructuring that always has a double edge. Each innovation simultaneously requires a new cohort of creative "knowledge workers" who, in the very process of developing new innovations, bring about, albeit indirectly, the routinization of the work of others. "Upskilling" therefore goes hand in hand with "downskilling," and new forms of specialization accompany the development of increasingly generic activities. Arguments about whether the development of an ever more technologically complex capitalism results in de-skilling or re-skilling are therefore beside the point. Skill does not just have a double-edged character for labor, it has an equally ambiguous meaning for employers. The innovation process that forms the necessary motor of change for capitalist development is deeply contradictory in its need for skill. Before a task can be automated, it is necessary to draw on the expertise and experience of someone who knows exactly how to do it, to anatomize every step in the process and work out how it can be standardized and how a machine can be programmed, or a less skilled worker trained to repeat these steps. Once expropriated, the knowledge and experience, or "craft," of these workers can be dispensed with, and cheaper, less skilled workers substituted to operate the new machines or administer the new systems.

We can therefore see the pool of intellectual workers as a diverse group, whose members at any given time play different roles in the economy. There are new groups in emergence, created as a result of new divisions between "head" and "hands" arising from the automation and/or de-skilling of traditional craft-based activities. In addition to various technical tasks, this includes people involved in the training and management of manual workers, as well as the "customer service" workers who could be said to be involved in the training and management of the general public. Then there are people involved in the invention, design, and testing of new products and processes or in customizing them for new applications. There are also people whose role is connected with the governance of the system or mediation between the various different parts of it. And there are people whose work involves providing content for a wide range of products and services, and communicating with, caring for, educating, informing, distracting, and entertaining the population. Although some of these roles are strongly delineated by the need for specific professional qualifications, technical knowledge, or less explicit structures of inclusion and exclusion, the boundaries between many are shifting and fluid. The very processes of change taking place mean that it is increasingly common for people to switch between public and private sector employment and to be required to exhibit an increasingly convergent range of "skills," "abilities," and "competencies" ranging from the use of standard software packages to "being a good team-player" or possessing "good time management skills."

The processes of standardization and the introduction of new management methods also contribute to some commonality of experience as many of these functions are themselves subjected to processes whereby the knowledge of the workers is expropriated and incorporated into computer programs or databases so that the tasks can be carried out by fewer, or less-skilled workers. In this category, for instance, we could include the knowledge of university lecturers who are asked to convert their lectures into content for standardized eLearning courses. The transformation of tacit knowledge into codified knowledge is a crucial part of this process. The question of who this knowledge belongs to thus becomes critical. If it is the property of individual workers, this places limits on the extent to which it can be appropriated. It is no accident that intellectual property rights are as strongly contested in the twenty-first century as land rights were in eighteenth-century Scotland.

Insofar as it involves the expropriation of their knowledge and its incorporation into knowledge databases, teaching materials, or cultural products, what is happening to intellectual workers now is not different *in kind* to what happened to craft weavers when their skills were incorporated into Jacquard weaving machines in the early nineteenth century. What is distinctly different, however, is the much broader and more diffuse nature of their occupational identities. It is, perhaps, in the nature of "knowledge work" that the worker does not expect to be doing the same thing over and over again but expects to progress either vertically, within the same organization or profession, or horizontally to other activities within the broader category of mental labor, which is, at least numerically, continuing to expand, even though many of the workers in it may be being de-skilled. It is, in other words, much harder to identify who are the winners and who the losers from change processes. Indeed, it may often be the case that the gains and losses are so intermingled that it is difficult for any individual worker to determine what the net effect has been.

Complex trade-offs are involved here: working longer hours in exchange for more autonomy in determining when you work them; shedding some administrative tasks in exchange for more travelling to meet customers; being given your own unit to manage in exchange for being moved into a different department under a less congenial senior manager; giving up your intellectual property rights in exchange for the chance to do more cutting-edge research; earning more in exchange for agreeing to meet certain targets; slightly reducing your teaching hours in exchange for teaching much larger classes. The impacts of these developments are contradictory and differentiated so we cannot draw large conclusions that life is necessarily getting worse across the board for all intellectual workers. At any given time, some may be upskilled while others are downskilled, some jobs may become more creative and autonomous while others are being routinized. Nevertheless, there is mounting evidence of some trends that seem to be increasing across a broad range of these activities.

The first is a general intensification of work. There is a lot of evidence, for instance from various European surveys of working conditions, working time, and quality of life,[16] that working hours are increasing and stress levels mounting across a range of white-collar jobs. Recent studies in universities have consistently shown that academics are overworked, overextended, and often on the point of burnout. One study in Canada by Janice Newson and Heather Menzies[17] looked not just at how many hours academics are working, including at home and in the evenings and weekends, but also at the demands on their time, including new reporting requirements, the shift to self-service administration, the need to fund-raise for research, and the need to meet rising expectations for immediate email responses from students, administration, and local and global academic colleagues. They found that not only are a sizeable number suffering from headaches, insomnia, memory lapses, and other symptoms of stress, but most are also increasingly incapable of functioning as public intellectuals. When asked whether they were reading as deeply and reflectively as they used to, 64 percent said no, and 79 percent said they were not reading as much as they would like. A sizable minority (42 percent) reported that their capacity for original and creative thinking in writing or in the classroom was fading. "I can't slow down enough to think" was a typical comment. Communication with colleagues also suffered. The authors conclude: "There is a dangerous suggestion here that the knowledge production academics are participating in is becoming less a process of knowing that emerges from themselves in ongoing dialogue with colleagues and, increasingly, is instead becoming a more fragmented process centred in remote knowledge systems, with academics themselves acting more as its extensions."

A second tendency—by no means unique to intellectual work—is for employment to become increasingly precarious. In the private sector this is evidenced by a growth in fixed-term contracts and, in some industries, in self-employment. Even where workers have permanent jobs, they are aware that they may be threatened at any moment by a merger or takeover or some other form of corporate restructuring. The increasingly generic nature of the skills required, in combination with the use of information and communications technologies to deliver work remotely, have resulted in the development of what is, in effect, a global reserve army of white-collar workers. Even if a job is not moved to India or China, the fear that it might be acts as a powerful disciplinary force on labor. Another source of job insecurity is the development of new kinds of internal labor markets within large companies related to the increasing use of project work. Instead of having a permanent job, workers are, in effect if not in name, employed on a project-by-project basis. When one project comes to an end, it is necessary to be picked for the next (normally on the basis of a CV posted on an internal company website). Failure to be picked can put your future with the company at risk. The public sector is not immune from these developments. Outsourcing can involve a shift of work to another location leading to actual redundancies, or a transfer of personnel leading to a change for those workers from a public to a private employer. In addition, of course, the public sector is itself an employer of casualized workers, whether these are agency nurses, lecturers paid by the session, or researchers employed on fixed-term contracts for the duration of a particular project.

A third trend is an intensification of the conflict between competition and collaboration. On the one hand, there has been an individualization of contracts leading to a breakdown of collective structures and solidarities; on the other—and in tension with it—there is an increasing requirement for team working. The standardization of processes I referred to earlier has produced a situation where each individual is now exposed to the highly contradictory requirement to simultaneously demonstrate both sameness and difference. On the one hand, there is a need to give up autonomy and creativity and perform according to the ever more stringent standards laid down from above (defined in terms of protocols, performance targets, and quality standards). The anonymous ways in which performance is measured usually mean that only that which is specified is credited. No recognition can be given for any extra value added by personal qualities that nobody thought to design indicators for in the system. On the other hand, there is an increasing need to be competitive and to stand out from the crowd. The process of form-filling becomes an expression of this contradiction, and camaraderie, idea sharing, and mutual support may become its victims. As I said earlier, this cannot be blamed simply on structural factors. Bureaucratic processes are produced and reproduced in a complicated and dynamic interaction between demands from above for efficiency and control and demands from below for fairness and transparency. And tensions between competitiveness and collaborativeness exist wherever human beings have to share scarce resources. Nevertheless, the evidence is that these conflicts are intensifying.

A fourth tendency that is visible, especially in the public sector, is a change in the relationship between workers who provide a service and the people who receive it. When a service is provided directly to a user only for what Marx would have called its "use value," then it is possible for the worker to be motivated directly by what, in an updating of Weber's ideas, Scandinavian feminists would call "care rationality." Thus teachers want their pupils to learn, nurses want their patients to be comfortable and get better, cooks want people to enjoy the food they prepare, and so on. Once a process has been standardized and commodified, even if it remains under public ownership the logic under which the work is done is changed. Though there may well be a "mission statement" declaring, for instance, that Pret à Manger is "passionate about food" or the Odeon cinema "fanatical about film" or even the London Metropolitan University "committed to social justice," the reality is that what Weber would have called "economic" or "institutional" motivation has taken over to a greater or lesser extent from motivation that is more ethical or affective. Even if the workers still care personally about the people they serve, they are no longer able to express this freely in the way that they serve them. Their work processes are determined by the need to follow the standard protocols and meet their targets. If the work has been transferred to the private sector from the public, then the ultimate overriding aim is to maximize profitability, even if this is moderated by intermediate demands. Examples of these might be the need to meet the specifications laid down in the contract with the public sector client or to achieve high customer satisfaction ratings or expand market share. It is one thing to wish someone a nice day because you happen to feel in a good mood and feel warm toward them; it is quite another to do it because it is in the standard script and you might be sacked if you don't.

The impacts of these four trends can be observed, to a greater or lesser extent, in many organizations, but what is their cumulative effect at a societal level? Here I would like to draw attention to three general social phenomena to which I believe these processes have contributed.

The first of these is the demise of the independent intellectual. This is a phenomenon that certainly cannot be blamed only on the commodification processes I have been describing and has to be placed in a much broader historical context. Indeed, the very notion of an independent intellectual is quite recent, and specific to certain cultures and milieux. As Virginia Woolf pointed out in 1929,[18] it was an identity that was largely restricted to people with an independent income and a private space and leisure in which to write—mainly men of the bourgeoisie. In the same year, Antonio Gramsci started developing in his prison notebooks a much broader concept of the intellectual, encompassing a range of people engaged in paid mental work, and posited the idea that it would be possible for "organic intellectuals" to emerge from the working class and develop a counter-hegemonic view of society.[19] During the next decade, there was a growth, at least in most large cities of the developed world, in what might be termed an alternative intellectual culture, often characterized as "bohemianism," still largely bourgeois in origin but sustained economically by a variety of means including journalism, work in the nascent mass media (especially the cinema and public broadcasting), small publishing houses, theaters and art galleries, as well as more traditional means such as the patronage of the rich and employment in universities. In the United States, state funding for the arts played an important role under Roosevelt's New Deal, as of course it did, in a very different way, in the Soviet Union.

In retrospect, it is the period following the Second World War that can be seen as a golden age of the independent intellectual, as it was for so many other social institutions (including full employment, the family wage, and various aspects of the welfare state). In Britain, there was not only a commitment to government funding for the arts, but also to expanding and democratizing higher education. By the later 1960s, when my generation came to adulthood, although intellectual life was still dominated by white bourgeois men, there were a number of places where, if they were determined enough and educated—and if they were female, childless—people could survive economically while functioning as independent intellectuals. One of these spaces was created by the slack in the relatively generous welfare state. It was possible (just) to survive on welfare benefits especially if one was lucky enough to have one's housing subsidized. Various forms of social cadging, including squatting and hitchhiking, were also practiced. These are long gone as viable strategies. A more respectable means of survival was to work in the voluntary sector where there was still scope for radicalism, experimentation, and independent thinking. This too is now gone as an option, as the voluntary sector has become professionalized, bureaucratized, and turned increasingly into an arm's-length extension of the state, filling the gaps created by cuts in statutory services. A third option was to work in the media, still, in that period, either mainly state-run (in the case of radio and television) or, in the case of "serious" publishing, dominated by small or medium-sized firms that could distribute their products through a network of independent bookshops. The mass media empires we see now were already there and already dominant in some sectors, including recorded music and newspapers, but it was possible still to make some sort of a living from freelance writing and reviewing for weekly journals, producing radio or television scripts, or working in publicly subsidized theaters or galleries. Again, this is no longer the case except for a relatively small minority skilled in the arts of begging and bragging. The income to be derived from, say, writing a book review for a serious weekly magazine is many times lower in terms of its buying power than it was forty years ago. How has this come about? In part it is undoubtedly an effect of the dominance of the media by a small number of very large transnational corporations with access to a global workforce for the more routine work. In my research I have come across examples of this such as editorial work for academic journals being done in India, graphic design in Malaysia, and animation in Vietnam. However, this need to compete in a global labor market is by no means the only factor. The decline in the real income to be derived from work in the media is also linked very directly with developments in a fourth place where independent intellectuals used to flourish: the universities.

One of the effects of the introduction of standardized performance measures into higher education has been a ratcheting up of the pressure to publish. In order to gain tenure, to receive research grants, to be promoted, to earn the discretionary portion of one's salary that is linked to performance measures, or to obtain a high research rating, it is necessary to publish, publish and then publish some more. If your offerings are rejected by the leading peer-reviewed journals in your field, start a new sub-field with some like-minded colleagues and create your own journal. If you have finished a piece of research, why condense the results into a single article when with luck you can squeeze three or four out of it? With each generation of scholars, the journals (and the sub-disciplines) multiply, and the number of published articles grows exponentially. And these are writers who write, literally, for nothing. Imagine what it is like to be a freelance writer trying to compete with them. Homeworkers sewing tee-shirts are working in a global market in which the competitors are women and children in places like Indonesia paid less than a dollar a day, but at least they are earning a wage, however low. But how is it possible to compete against free labor? And with the market so flooded, how is it possible for a book even produced for love to get noticed? I have already spoken about the way in which the commodification of higher education has reduced the time and freedom of academics to play the role of public intellectual. It has also hastened the death of independent intellectual life outside the academy, crowding out of the public space the sort of book that could still be published in the 1960s and 1970s—the intelligent nonfiction paperback written for a non-specialist lay audience, exemplified in those turquoise-covered Pelicans that used to dapple the bookshelves of anyone with any pretension to an intellectual life.

The second phenomenon I would like to discuss is the impact of these developments on ethical and professional codes of behavior. I have already mentioned the way in which we are increasingly expected to violate the injunctions "Thou shalt not beg" and "Thou shalt not brag." There is also growing pressure to disobey the commandment "Thou shalt not steal" when it comes to one's neighbor's intellectual property. I am not just referring here to out-and-out plagiarism but to those subtler forms of theft that include stealing ideas, failing to acknowledge sources, and selective citation. This is not always done out of malice. More usually it arises from a combination of pressure of time, pressure of competition, and the ease with which new technologies allow one to cut and paste from existing work. But the effect is to destroy solidarity and to create an atmosphere of suspicion and secrecy that is the enemy of collegiality and, incidentally, also of good teaching. Environments are being created where it is more and more difficult to behave with generosity, modesty, and integrity and harder and harder to build those "intellectual collectives" that Pierre Bourdieu saw as so essential for developing a critique of the prevailing norms, developing models of social alternatives, and "defending us against symbolic domination, increasingly backed by the authority of science."[20]

Finally, I would like to point to a third impact of these developments. This is the contradiction that lies right at the core of the capitalist development process: its insatiable need for innovative and creative thinkers. As science and technology become ever more complex, as the speed of change accelerates, as global competitiveness becomes more cutthroat, and as the world's demands for education, training, information, and entertainment grow exponentially, there is an ever-increasing need for people who can think, as the cliché puts it, "outside the box"—who can see how the parts fit into the whole and how the whole could be redesigned, who can, in short, critique what is there, imagine alternatives, and plan and implement changes. But the practices of "knowledge management" that are developed to control them produce conditions that are inimical to that very creativity. Penned into little steel cages, the geese may stop laying their golden eggs. But allowed to fly free they might start to see what lies beyond the farm gates and hanker for change. In the resolution of this dilemma we might see the greatest hope for the future.

4. The Globalization of Labor and the Role of National Governments

Toward a Conceptual Framework

It is generally agreed that we are in the midst of a major global restructuring of industry, enabled by a series of interconnected factors. A first factor has been the opening up of world markets with the creation, since the political developments of 1989, of what is now more or less a global market for both goods and services. A second factor has been a strong concentration of capital, leading to the increasing dominance of many market sectors by a relatively small number of large transnational corporations. A third factor has been the spread of digital and communications technologies that not only make it possible to redistribute spatially activities that were formerly rooted to a single location but also to put in place mechanisms whereby these activities can be centrally coordinated and remotely managed in real time. Finally, neoliberal government policies have removed many of the institutional barriers to restructuring: for instance, by opening up infrastructure to the market, removing barriers to the import and export of goods, services, information, and capital (though not to the free movement of people), and deregulating labor markets.

Though these changes are widely recognized, there is surprisingly little information on their precise nature and extent. For instance, there has been widespread public panic in some countries, such as the United States, about the threat of "offshore outsourcing" to local jobs, but there are no reliable data on the numbers or types of jobs affected, either in the regions from which they are supposed to have disappeared or in the regions to which they are supposed to have migrated.

One reason for this lacuna is a lack of evidence, due to the inadequacy of the existing categories used to classify industries and jobs. The units of analysis traditionally used by statisticians—"enterprises," "sectors," and "occupations"—have proved to be inadequate to describe the recent changes, not least because each of these units has itself been undergoing transformation. Take the concept of the "enterprise." In a period characterized by rapid mergers and de-mergers, strategic alliances, the dominance of "brands" in determining corporate identity, large-scale outsourcing, and multiplication of contractual forms of employment, it is becoming increasingly problematic to define what the boundaries might be of any particular firm. It is a similar story with the "sector" in a situation in which there has been rapid convergence between many traditional sectors while new sectors emerge continuously, not just to produce new categories of goods but also to supply on an outsourced basis services that were traditionally provided internally. Finally, the category "occupation" has become increasingly unstable in a situation in which workers are expected to change their skills in response to each wave of technological and institutional innovation.

The existing categories derive, of course, from traditional frameworks that historically provided a useful means to analyze national economies and, to a lesser extent, to compare one national economy with another. They are firmly embedded in national and international institutional practices and cannot easily be jettisoned either by policymakers or by serious scholars seeking to understand the seismic economic changes currently under way and their associated social and political impacts.

Nevertheless, it is clear that there is a need for an alternative conceptual framework that will make it possible to model these changes and develop indicators that will enable trends to be monitored in the future, both to understand changes over time and to enable comparisons between different countries and regions. Such a framework could offer us a basis for understanding the dynamics of restructuring.

In this essay, I propose the basis for a conceptual framework for analyzing the restructuring of industry in both its spatial and legal dimensions and identifying the tendencies that are likely to shape future trends. But if we are to understand the full impact on employment and delineate the contours of the new global division of labor that is emerging, such a structural analysis only provides half the story: it is not only necessary to understand the logic of the restructuring of capital; it is also necessary to understand the forms of resistance (or encouragement) that this restructuring encounters, the ways that these are mediated institutionally in any given context, and the ways that this process of negotiation between global economic forces on the one hand, and social and political actors at national and regional levels on the other, serve to shape the eventual outcome. State institutions, as part of this mediation process, may play a crucial role in determining the new industrial geography.

However, the state is also implicated in the current process of restructuring in another way: it forms a new field for expansion for capital.[1] I discuss in chapter 6 in this collection the role played by the commodification of public services and administrative processes in contributing to the emergence of new multinational corporations and the growth of existing ones and how this, in turn, drives the further development of restructuring. This should not be forgotten in any discussion of the changing relationship between national governments and transnational corporations.

IN THE CURRENT LITERATURE, there are three main ways of thinking about the interrelationship between different industrial units. These are the "value chain" or "commodity chain,"[2] the "filière,"[3] and the "network."[4] Each of these approaches has strengths and weaknesses from the point of view of helping to develop a framework for comprehending the full scope of the restructuring that is currently taking place.

The "value chain" offers a strong metaphor for understanding the linear relationship between inputs and outputs in the supply chains that produce specific commodities. Developed primarily for the purpose of understanding manufacturing industries, it is framed sectorally, illustrating each stage in the production and distribution of a given product, and enabling us to understand not only the spatial distribution of the tasks that contribute to producing the final product and the value contributed in each step but also the power relationships between the different actors along the chain. However, it is much weaker as a tool for understanding the lateral flows between sectors, or for modeling economy-wide interconnections within a particular territory.

By contrast, the "filière"—literally a "thread" or "filament," but also conceived as a "flow" from one sphere of economic activity to another—provides us with a very strong concept for understanding flows across whole economies, in particular ways for modeling inputs and outputs between primary, secondary, and tertiary sectors. It can, for instance, help us visualize how a product like electricity or water is distributed across an economy. However, it is a weaker tool for understanding international flows, which affect only parts of local economies. Compared with the "chain" metaphor, it also makes it rather difficult to study the power relationships between different industrial actors and their internal governance structures.

The "network" metaphor, so beloved by proponents of the "knowledge-based economy," provides the potential for sophisticated modeling of the complex horizontal interactions between multiple actors, both within and between international territories. However, it tells us almost nothing about the direction of flows between them and fails to provide any framework for analyzing the power relations between them. This makes it extremely difficult to use this metaphor to understand the drivers of change.

If we are to develop a framework that overcomes these weaknesses, it is necessary to delve more deeply and uncover the assumptions that underlie these three models and have contributed to the formation of the three contrasting metaphors (chains, flows, and networks). It is my contention that a common underlying logic can be observed underpinning all three of these approaches, a logic that has its intellectual roots in the European Enlightenment of the eighteenth century. Four theoretical concepts come together to create this logic.

These are, first, the theory of the *division of labor,* developed by Adam Smith;[5] second, the *labor theory of value,* also found in Smith, later modified by others including Marx;[6] third, the theory of *comparative advantage,* again found in Smith, and modified by Ricardo;[7] and fourth, the concept of an economy as based on *inputs and outputs between different economic classes,* chronologically the earliest of these ideas, developed by Quesnay in 1758.[8]

Taken together, these give us a five-part model.

The first component of this model proposes that "businesses" are broken down into "trades," "branches," or "functions." To quote Smith:

> The division of labor, however, so far as it can be introduced, occasions, in every art, a proportionable increase of the productive powers of labor. The separation of different trades and employments from one another seems to have taken place in consequence of this advantage.[9]

According to the second component, *the more specialist the division of labor the more value is added in each operation.* To quote Smith again:

> The value which the workmen add to the materials, therefore, resolves itself . . . into two parts, of which the one pays their

> wages, the other the profits of their employer upon the whole stock of materials and wages which he advanced. He could have no interest to employ them, unless he expected from the sale of their work something more than what was sufficient to replace his stock to him; and he could have no interest to employ a great stock rather than a small one, unless his profits were to bear some proportion to the extent of his stock.[10]

Smith is clear that the value of a final product is not just constituted by the added value of each stage of the manufacturing process but also includes value added by inputs of services:

> In the price of flour or meal, we must add to the price of the corn, the profits of the miller, and the wages of his servants; in the price of bread, the profits of the baker, and the wages of his servants; and in the price of both, the labor of transporting the corn from the house of the farmer to that of the miller, and from that of the miner to that of the baker, together with the profits of those who advance the wages of that labor.[11]

The third component proposes that *the comparative advantages of regions make it profitable to introduce a spatial dimension to the division of labor.* Here, we may quote Ricardo:

> Under a system of perfectly free commerce, each country naturally devotes its capital and labor to such employments as are most beneficial to each. . . . It is this principle which determines that wine shall be made in France and Portugal, that corn shall be grown in America and Poland, and that hardware and other goods shall be manufactured in England. . . .
>
> If Portugal had no commercial connexion with other countries, instead of employing a great part of her capital and industry in the production of wines, with which she purchases for her own use the cloth and hardware of other countries, she

> would be obliged to devote a part of that capital to the manufacture of those commodities, which she would thus obtain probably inferior in quality as well as quantity.[12]

Nevertheless, this comparative advantage may be constrained by limits to the free operation of markets and movements of capital and of labor. Like his neoliberal British followers at the beginning of the twenty-first century, Smith discussed this in relation to "the policy of Europe." To quote him again:

> The policy of Europe, by not leaving things at perfect liberty, occasions other inequalities of much greater importance.
>
> It does this chiefly in the three following ways. First, by restraining the competition in some employments to a smaller number than would otherwise be disposed to enter into them; secondly, by increasing it in others beyond what it naturally would be; and, thirdly, by obstructing the free circulation of labor and stock, both from employment to employment and from place to place.[13]

Linked to the third proposition is a fourth, that *centralized governance is necessary to ensure that the division of labor is coordinated and value extracted.*

Finally, if we are to see the picture from the perspective of the economy as a whole, rather than that of the individual capitalist, it must be noted that, though each individual "business" organizes its internal division of labor along the above lines, it is necessary to see the general assemblage of all businesses as *interconnected through a flow of inputs and outputs of goods and services traded across the whole economy.* In other words, we have to envisage a national economy as consisting of the sum of these flows of inputs and outputs as first modeled in the prototype flow table (*Tableau Ėconomique)* for the French economy developed by Quesnay, the remote ancestor of the input-output tables that now form part of the national accounts of most countries.

This concept of *flows* is also extremely useful for modeling the interrelationships between different units in the division of labor: each unit can be seen as receiving *inputs* (in the form of raw materials, goods, or services), either from an external source or from another unit within the business to which it *adds value* before transmitting it in the form of an *output* either to another unit or to an end customer.

In order to produce this model, Quesnay analyzed the economy using a *functional* approach, distinguishing between activities that produced value (in "the productive sector") and those that did not (in "the sterile sector") and breaking down the population into generic *classes.* Three basic groups are identified: farmers, landlords, and artisans, but the division of labor in his model introduces additional categories: laborers, who add value by making inputs of labor; and merchants, who provide the means to make inputs of foreign goods and raw materials. These groups are *generic* in the sense that they are defined only in terms of their function in the economy, not in terms of the particular products or services they grow, make, or trade in, or the types of property from which they receive rent. This functional approach can also be discerned in Marx's analysis of the division of labor and insistence on the contributions to the production of value of all those workers, whether manual or non-manual, who are involved in any way in the production of any given commodity:

> The different labor capacities which cooperate together to form the productive machine as a whole contribute in very different ways to the direct process by which the commodity, or, more appropriate here, the product, is formed, one working more with his hands, another more with his brain, one as a **manager**, **engineer** or technician, etc., another as an **overlooker**, the third directly as a manual worker, or even a mere assistant, more and more of the *functions of labor capacity* are included under the direct concept of *productive labor*, and their repositories under the concept of *productive workers.*[14]

The functional differentiation here is much greater than in Quesnay—not least, perhaps, because of the technical advances in production that had taken place in the meanwhile—but the functions are nevertheless described in *generic* terms.

Taken together, then, these principles give us the skeleton for a theoretical framework for understanding the logic underpinning the new global division of labor and the interconnectedness of economies, both laterally, across territories through "networks" between firms and "flows" across whole economies, and vertically, along "chains" that connect suppliers to their customers both locally and internationally. The functional approach that underpins this model suggests that the best way to conceptualize the basic unit of this structure is as a generic business function.

If we take the generic function as a basic unit, it is possible to conceptualize a chain, or a network, or a flow, or indeed a whole national economy, as composed of multiples of these basic units, or modules, capable of being interconnected in a number of different ways. The more standardized these individual components are, the greater the range of different ways in which they can potentially be reconfigured. Just as it is possible to imagine electrical current either as particles or waves, so it is equally possible to imagine these economic units either as separate components (for instance as Lego bricks) or as parts of a continuous flow. Which metaphor is most useful depends, perhaps, on the specific nature of the commodity under discussion: whether, for instance, it is a material object that is assembled from components that have to be physically transported from one location to another, or whether it is a substance that is provided in a continuous metered flow (such as water or electricity) or a service supplied across telecommunications networks. Regardless of the metaphor used, the underlying logic of interconnection remains the same.

However, if we want to understand the process by which change comes about—in other words, the process by which these interconnections are reconfigured or become more elaborated over time—it is necessary to go one step further, below the level of the business function, right down to the individual task, and the labor process of the worker who carries it out—the basic components, so to speak, of these blocks or flows. Here we can draw on Frederick Winslow Taylor[15] and Harry Braverman[16] for conceptual insights.

For Taylor, the basic unit of analysis was the *task*. Indeed, he went so far as to say that "every single act of every workman can be reduced to a science."

> Perhaps the most prominent single element in modern scientific management is the task idea. The work of every workman is fully planned out by the management at least one day in advance, and each man receives in most cases complete written instructions, describing in detail the task which he is to accomplish, as well as the means to be used in doing the work. And the work planned in advance in this way constitutes a task which is to be solved, as explained above, not by the workman alone, but in almost all cases by the joint effort of the workman and the management. This task specifies not only what is to be done but how it is to be done and the exact time allowed for doing it.[17]

Braverman also used the *task* as the basic unit of analysis, but viewed changes in work organization from the perspective of labor, and the societal division of labor, rather than from the perspective of the business (although he drew strongly, if critically, on the management science literature in order to do so). He also highlighted the crucial role in bringing about these changes of workers' skills on the one hand, and technology on the other (again echoing both Smith and Taylor). Although also using a *functional* analysis, Braverman developed the term *labor process* (rather than the more management-oriented *business process*) to describe the unit of analysis for analyzing changes in the organization of work. Though the two concepts are distinctly different, emerging as they do from different scientific paradigms, there are nevertheless interesting parallels between them, with the restructuring of business processes being accompanied by the restructuring of labor processes, the introduction of new technologies being accompanied by the need for new skills, the standardization of tasks being accompanied by the routinization of work, and so on. Bringing together insights from the management literature with those derived from the study of labor processes provides a useful framework for understanding the mechanisms of work restructuring, which, in turn, creates a basis for the analysis of value chain restructuring.

Drawing on Braverman's analysis of the ways in which workers' tasks are systematized and standardized enables us to posit a simplified model of the process by which tasks become redesigned to enable them to be converted into the basic modules that make up the building blocks of global value chains/filières/networks.

In the first stage, workers' *tacit knowledge*[18] is *made explicit and codified.* This codification allows for a *standardization* of tasks, which takes place in the second stage. Third, this in turn makes it possible for outputs to be *quantified and measured.* Once this has taken place, a fourth stage becomes possible, in which workers can be *managed by results.* This means that management no longer needs to take place in "real" time and space but can be carried out remotely. This spatial and temporal displacement in turn makes possible a variety of different forms of *business disaggregation,* in a fifth stage, for the work to be reorganized, either *spatially* (by relocating it to another site) or *contractually* (by outsourcing it) or both.

Work processes are, in effect, modularized, and this modularization makes possible a wide range of different spatial and contractual permutations and combinations: aggregation or disaggregation; centralization or decentralization; labor processes based on single tasks or multiple tasks. The modularization of employment does not necessarily lead to any given outcome in terms of relocation or outsourcing; rather, it multiplies the options available to employers for spatial and contractual organization.[19]

In recent years, services have increasingly become commodified and subject to their own internal processes of standardization, fragmentation, and the introduction of a spatial division of labor just as manufacturing industries were in the past. The scale of outsourcing is now sufficiently great for new sectors that supply outsourced business services to be detectable in the statistics. The companies in these new sectors are developing their own internal patterns of spatial and contractual disaggregation, leading to further elaboration of the global division of labor. As the increasingly generic nature of services extends the possibilities for modularization, major new multinationals are emerging to supply standardized services on an outsourced basis—often many times larger than the public or private sector organizations that are their customers.[20]

SO FAR, I HAVE presented a schematic overview of the logic of global industrial restructuring. Of course, in the real world companies, however global, do not have things all their own way. Economic development takes place in preexisting landscapes where workers and their practices have been historically and culturally shaped by a variety of different institutions. The particular form that work takes in any given place is therefore a product of an encounter between global and local forces.

It is common to see the state and global capital as the two main protagonists in this ongoing process of negotiation. An extensive body of literature since 1990 has tried to characterize the relationship between them and how it has changed over the period that began with the "Fordist" postwar compromise (bolstered by the politics of the Cold War), continued during the bumpy crises of the 1970s, and succumbed to what is generally regarded as a global neoliberal consensus after 1989. Have the forces of globalization swept all before them, creating a world map in which, in Kenichi Ohmae's words, as far as "real flows of financial and industrial activity are concerned . . . borders have largely disappeared"?[21] Has the state become a mere "transmission belt from the global to the national economy" as Robert Cox contends?[22] Or is its role more ambivalent than that, acting as a "mediator," as Leo Panitch[23] puts it, or "orchestrator" as David Coates[24] describes it, of the relationship between global capital and local labor?

Framing the problem in this way is productive for many purposes, but it can leave the impression of the "state" as an abstract and undifferentiated entity, rendering invisible the enormous differences that exist between states: with the hegemonic power of the United States at one extreme and at the other "failed states," or those that cannot even guarantee a rule of law sufficient to enforce the most basic labor standards.[25] Supranational bodies play a part. The World Trade Organization (WTO), for instance, plays a role in forcing open markets, and the International Labor Organization (ILO) attempts to establish minimum labor standards. In recent years, regional groupings like Mercosur in South America and the European Union (EU) in Europe have also tried to shape employment within their regions. The EU's famous 2000 Lisbon declaration was a particularly striking example of this. However, its goal of making the EU "the most competitive and dynamic knowledge-based economy in the world capable of sustainable economic growth with more and better jobs and greater social cohesion" contained many internal contradictions. For instance, it is very hard to pursue the goal of competitiveness without downward pressure on wages and working conditions. This militates against jobs becoming "better." Similarly, the pursuit of dynamism is likely to create forms of instability that make it more difficult to achieve "greater social cohesion." Such examples could be multiplied. What is clear is that the policies based on such strategies form an extra intervening layer in the relationship between global capital and local labor. But it is also clear that they do not substitute for the national level: the outcomes of the same global strategies may still be substantially different between countries even within the same bloc. And these outcomes—positive or negative—will have very concrete consequences for workers as well as shaping corporate decisions about what function to locate where.

It is important to bear in mind that national and supranational policies are not the only shaping forces. Any employment relationship is also molded by a complex interconnecting mesh of social, cultural, political, and economic forces, many with deep historical roots. These include taken-for-granted assumptions about, for instance, what is appropriate behavior for a man or a woman, relationships between different ethnic, religious, or linguistic groups, and ethical codes. They also include the traditional industrial structure of a region, which is in turn influenced by its geography and history: whether, for instance, a regional economy has relied on fishing, mining, agriculture, or production industry; whether it has large cities built on trade or the exploitation of colonies; whether it was itself a colony; or how early it was industrialized.

These and other factors have contributed to the development of specific patterns of division of labor in which some groups of workers have been able to develop forms of bargaining power based on their skills or social status that have enabled them to negotiate some degree of protection and relatively favorable rewards and conditions. To the extent that these groups are still able to wield this power, they remain a force to be reckoned with, a force whose services cannot be offered unconditionally on a plate by their governments to predatory multinational corporations, however desperate the need for jobs. In many occupations and industries this power is under threat from global reserve armies whose work can substitute for theirs, either by moving the jobs to another country or by importing migrant workers to carry them out, or a combination of both, but, even so, its achievements cannot be dismantled overnight because it has historically contributed to the construction of a range of institutions that are firmly embedded in the national fabric. The power of organized labor (or its absence), whether expressed through trade unions or political parties, has played a part in determining the specific form that institutions take in a country, including its vocational training, labor laws, national insurance, health and welfare, and industrial relations systems. In each country, a particular bargain has been struck between capital and labor, but the specific form this compromise has taken has been historically shaped, with the power of organized labor playing a role in this process.

The need to understand how this varies from country to country has received a strong impetus from the most recent wave of global restructuring of capital, and with it the restructuring of labor processes, skills, occupational identities, and employment contracts over the last two decades. Considerable scholarly attention has been given to analyzing the different "varieties of capitalism"[26] or "worlds of welfare capitalism"[27] in an attempt to find meaningful patterns. It is not my task here to summarize this literature. Rather, my aim is to draw attention to the fact that any conceptual model of global industrial restructuring will have to take into account a differentiated analysis of the role played by national policy in shaping corporate practices and in attracting (or repelling) inward investment. This analysis will need to be differentiated along two dimensions: first, a differentiation between different types of state that takes into account their power relative to global corporations; and second, a differentiation between the role of national governments and that of other institutions in shaping the encounter between capital and labor in any given territory. This too varies considerably between countries and regions.

This project is of more than scholarly interest. If it can be demonstrated that particular institutional forms are associated with outcomes that are better (or worse) for workers, then we can draw the conclusion that policy can make a difference. Once this is established, then a purposeful quest can be embarked upon to find out which policies benefit which groups and develop strategies for pursuing (or thwarting) particular types of policy.

I HAVE ARGUED IN this essay that to understand the global restructuring of industry (and hence of work) currently taking place, it is necessary to develop a conceptual model in which economies are seen not as made up of "enterprises" within "sectors" but as aggregates of "business functions," which are in turn made up of increasingly interchangeable "tasks" carried out by workers using specific labor processes. It is these modularized tasks that make up the smallest units of the aggregate, and it is workers' knowledge, together with their bodily strength and dexterity, that therefore forms the basis of the whole edifice, however it is configured. This knowledge must be codified and standardized as a precondition for any new elaboration of the division of labor, whether this disaggregation takes a spatial or a contractual form (or both). The deconstruction and reconstruction of companies, sectors, and regional and national economies is thus integrally linked with the deconstruction and reconstruction of skills, labor processes, and occupational identities.

While such a model can provide an insight into the dynamics of the restructuring of capital, it cannot provide an understanding of the impact on employment without also taking into account another ingredient: the role of the state. This has to be considered in two distinct aspects: its role in attracting and controlling capital (as well as disciplining and reproducing labor) on its territory; and its role in opening up new fields for the expansion of capital. These roles are not necessarily in harmony with each other. Indeed, there are clear contradictions. For instance, there is a contradiction between the aim of a national government to attract foreign investment to its territory on the one hand, and the aim of reducing the cost of its public services by outsourcing them to global suppliers on the other. Under conditions of globalization, additional contradictions arise for national governments in relation to their historical roles in collecting taxes and in managing competition between MNEs. But these topics are beyond the scope of this essay and are questions for further investigation elsewhere.

5. Expression and Expropriation

The Dialectics of Autonomy and Control in Creative Labor

Creative labor occupies a highly contradictory position in modern, global, "knowledge-based" economies. On the one hand, companies have to balance their insatiable need for a stream of innovative ideas with the equally strong imperative to gain control over intellectual property and manage a creative workforce. On the other, creative workers have to find a balance between the urge for self-expression and recognition and the need to earn a living. The interplay between these antagonistic imperatives produces a complex set of relations, encompassing a variety of forms both of collusion and of conflict between managers, clients, and workers, with each action provoking a counterreaction in a dynamic movement that resembles an elaborate minuet, in which some steps follow formal conventions but new moves are constantly being invented.

This dialectical dance forms the subject of this article. The choice of topic is rooted in a general interest in the contradictory role of creative workers in the restructuring of global capital, a role that renders them simultaneously both complicit agents of restructuring and victims of it.[1] However, the immediate stimulus for the article was the results of some European research carried out by the WORKS (Work Organization Restructuring in the Knowledge Society) Project,[2] which carried out extensive research across the EU between 2005 and 2009. Alongside quantitative and theoretical analysis, this project carried out in-depth case studies on the impacts of value chain restructuring on work organization and the quality of working life across a range of industries[3] and occupational groups[4] and in contrasting national settings.

These studies uncovered major differences between countries, industries, and occupational groups. Nevertheless, some very striking common trends cut across all these variables, in particular, a noticeable standardization and intensification of work and a speed-up of its pace. Linked in many cases with a growing precariousness of work, these had strongly negative impacts not only on the quality of work but also on feelings of security and career prospects as well as on the quality of life outside the workplace, especially for people with children or other care responsibilities.[5] These results, which were confirmed by an analysis of the results of the European Working Conditions Survey,[6] were particularly pronounced among white-collar workers, who were being put under pressure from a number of different directions, including pressure to work to targets set by clients, respond directly to demands from customers, sometimes in different time zones, and exercise a growing range of communications and emotional skills on top of their core tasks.[7]

Despite the fact that a high proportion of the workers interviewed experienced these effects as negative and that many of the fifty-seven in-depth organizational case studies were carried out in companies and industries that were unionized, and quite a few in countries with a strong tradition of collective bargaining, at least in comparison to the United States or the United Kingdon (for example, Denmark, Sweden, Norway, Germany, Austria, Belgium, and the Netherlands), it was striking that there had been remarkably little resistance to these changes. As Pamela Meil, Per Tengblad, and Peter Docherty concluded, “Union or works council response was generally passive or reactive and focused mainly on dealing with the employment consequences of restructuring rather than influencing the shape of the new structure"; and "very few (if any) examples of representation influence the change itself. The management prerogative in defining restructuring seems almost total."[8]

The 300-odd workers interviewed in the thirty occupational case studies linked to the fifty-seven organizational case studies included a range of different groups of workers, some of whom might be regarded as having quite a bit of individual negotiating power with employers or clients (fashion designers, researchers in R&D for IT products, and software engineers), so it might be expected that some would resist in individualized and personal ways rather than collective ones. However, the interviews showed little evidence of this, either. In fact, software engineers, who might be supposed to be more individualistic than the manual or clerical workers also included in the study, provided the only instance of a strong collective response to restructuring, with one group of IT workers (in the UK) taking strike action in an attempt to resist outsourcing.[9]

In retrospect, this failure of "knowledge workers" to resist restructuring of their work even when they know it will be deleterious is one of the most surprising results of the whole project. Like the dog that failed to bark in the night in the Sherlock Holmes story, it provokes the question: "Why not?" What can account for this failure to resist these negative changes either individually or collectively?

It occurred to me that, although this question was not directly addressed in the WORKS research design, it might be productive to reexamine the rich mass of data from the project to see what light it could shed on the contradictory position of "creative" or "knowledge" workers in value chain restructuring. In particular, I wondered whether these results might illuminate the complex and dynamic interplay between management's drive to control the creative workforce and workers' urges for autonomy. This article is a first result of this process, looking at the results of the WORKS case studies but also drawing on some of my past research as well as work by other authors. It begins by outlining the role of knowledge workers in value chain restructuring. Then it looks at what is distinctive about "creative" knowledge-based work. It then moves on to a summary of current trends in the reorganization of knowledge work before embarking on an analysis of the multiple forms of control that operate in knowledge work and the ways in which their interactions might impede effective resistance to management imperatives. Finally, I draw some brief conclusions.

I have used the overlapping terms "knowledge worker" and "creative worker" somewhat interchangeably throughout, aware that neither is really adequate, especially when the knowledge that forms the content of the work and contributes to the occupational identities of many non-manual workers is undergoing a rapid process of commodification, degradation, and reconstruction. By discussing the role that creativity plays within "knowledge" work, as I do below, I hope to avoid too much terminological confusion.

THE ROLE OF CREATIVE WORKERS IN CAPITALIST DEVELOPMENT

It is more or less axiomatic, at least in a capitalist economic system, that growth depends on innovation. And the more global and competitive that system is, then the greater is the need for rapidity in this innovation. Since all innovation comes, ultimately, from human creativity, then creative workers are *ipso facto* integral to any development process.

This assertion is easily made, but distinguishing "creative workers" from the general crowd of the global labor force is by no means a simple task, such is the complexity and interconnectedness of the division of labor in which each activity is linked interdependently with so many others across spatial, temporal, and corporate boundaries.

There is a sense in which all economic activity requires human ingenuity and knowledge. Just as basic human needs—for food, shelter, warmth, etc.—have not really changed over millennia, neither have the tasks required to meet them. Human beings still extract and harvest the planet's natural resources, manipulate and recombine them, distribute them, consume them, and dispose of the waste, as well as care for and entertain each other. Back in the mists of time, no doubt, many of these activities were carried out by workers who were fairly autonomous and free to improvise within the constraints of the resources and time available to them. However, over the centuries diverse social systems have developed complex divisions of labor, usually strongly gendered and many involving hierarchical forms of control. In these divisions of labor those who give orders have removed much of the scope for creativity of those who follow these orders. Under capitalism, changes in this division of labor have been highly dynamic—a continuous, if uneven, process of decomposition and recomposition of sectors, organizations, labor processes, and skills, driven by the imperative of maximizing the extraction of value from any given unit of labor. In this process there has been an ongoing separation of tasks, in particular a separation of routine activities from those requiring initiative and imagination. Harry Braverman[10] analyzed and documented the use of the scientific management approach developed by Frederick Winslow Taylor in 1911[11] and its extension from the factory to office work[12] and introduced the concept of "de-skilling" as an essential component of this process, showing the ways in which the tacit knowledge of workers could be captured by managers, and analyzed, standardized, and mechanized to create simplified labor processes that could be carried out by less skilled (and hence cheaper) workers. Followers of Braverman have tended to emphasize this de-skilling aspect of the restructuring of labor processes. However, Braverman himself, like Taylor before him, made it clear that he regarded the separation of "mental" activities from "manual" ones as a process that also involved the creation of some new, more highly skilled activities.

There is a close connection between the simplification of routine tasks and expansion in the role of the manager. As Taylor, put it in the introduction to his book: "The management must take over and perform much of the work which is now left to the men; almost every act of the workman should be preceded by one or more preparatory acts of the management which enable him [*sic*] to do his work better and quicker than he otherwise could."

As the results of the past division of labor become increasingly embedded in technologies, social systems, and the physical infrastructure, and the current division of labor becomes more complex and geographically and contractually extended, there is often a separation between these "mental" and "manual" activities that makes it difficult to perceive their interconnections. When workers are in different companies, on different continents, linked only perhaps through a shared software platform, occasional meetings between intermediaries, or the presence of the same logo, the interdependence of their activities (and their shared origins in a previously integrated job description) are rendered invisible.

Nevertheless, it is difficult to understand the role of creative labor in the overall development process without some analysis of the interlinkages between the different components of global value chains. Only then does it become possible to gain an insight into the functional relationship between creative work and capitalist development and, in doing so, the contradictory pressures that shape and reshape creative work. This simultaneously generates new openings for innovation, and new skill sets associated with emerging technologies, while routinizing and de-skilling, or even rendering obsolete, older occupations.

What, then, are these roles, and what imperatives shape them?

One important creative function is the *invention of new products*. This can take place in several ways under advanced capitalism. One is simply to appropriate something that has traditionally been made using craft methods and devise a means of mass production for it. Another is to develop new products in the Research and Development (R&D) department of a company where the creative work is carried out by employees. Alternatively, the labor might be acquired from a freelancer, an independent entrepreneur, or smaller company (either voluntarily, through a subcontract, or involuntarily, through predatory acquisition). In yet another scenario, the research may be carried out in a university, subsidized from public or charitable funds, and then handed over to a private company for exploitation. In each of these situations, the relationship of the creator of the work to the company producing the final product will be different, as will his or her relationship to the ownership of the intellectual property in the creation. These specific conditions of ownership, control, and management will, directly or indirectly, influence the power relations between the parties and shape the working life of the creative worker in terms of income and autonomy.

Related to the function of developing new products is that of *customizing, improving, or adapting them for different purposes or different markets.* Once again, we have a wide range of possible relationships between these creative workers and capital, which may be governed by a range of different employment contracts, licensing agreements, or contracts for the supply of services. This category may be expanded to include a variety of activities involving more ephemeral *design and styling* (for example, of clothing or household goods).

Linked to the function of adapting and customizing products is that of *providing content* for various forms of media. Many such activities have their origins in traditional forms of art and entertainment, and the workers who produce them cover a vast range of occupations: writers, musicians, visual artists, film producers and technicians, graphic designers, translators, website designers, and many more, with solitary and introspective activities at one extreme and highly technical ones, requiring intensively interactive teamworking, at the other. These are, perhaps, the workers most people think of when the term "creative" is used. However, their activities are increasingly embedded in the global value chains of large companies or reliant on such companies for distribution or patronage and, although their relationships with these companies are perhaps even more varied than those described so far, it is difficult, if not impossible, to distinguish these workers clearly from other categories of worker in the same value chain.

Overlapping with these content-generating activities is another set of activities connected with *education, training, and providing information to the public.* Again, these are increasingly hard to isolate. As education and training become commodified, for example, there is a continuum between face-to-face teaching in real time, engaging in various distance-learning activities, or providing content for course materials delivered electronically. Similarly, the provision of government information, usage instructions for appliances, or customer service information by companies is increasingly likely to be delivered online or via a call center, with new divisions of labor between specialist authors at one extreme and de-skilled workers providing information from standard scripts at the other. In the past, it might have seemed logical to make a clear distinction between commercial information provision and the provision of information to citizens by the state (and regard the latter as part of the function of governance), but the commodification of public services and the growth in outsourcing them to the private sector or consigning them to the voluntary sector has rendered such a distinction increasingly anachronistic. Nevertheless, it remains the case that a considerable amount of creative labor is invested in the *legitimation and reproduction of the power of the state*, as well as *the reproduction of the workforce*, so creative work should not be regarded as solely concerned with the development and circulation of commodities for the market. Here too we find a variety of different relationships both to the intellectual property that is produced and to the employer, including the bureaucratic relationships of civil servants with the governments that employ them, more contingent employment relationships, including self-employment, and commercial contracts between companies, with the workers' output being regarded sometimes as a public good, sometimes as a product in its own right, and sometimes as a form of advertising.

My final category of creative work is even harder to delineate from other categories of labor, only in this case the blurred boundary is with management and technical functions. This is the creative labor that goes into *inventing new systems and processes or adapting old ones for new purposes.* Very often, these systems and processes involve the labor processes of other workers. Without this particular form of creativity, the current global division of labor could not exist. Christened "living think work" by Mike Hales,[13] this is the labor that analyzes the labor processes of others, works out how to standardize them, automate them, outsource them, manage them, and recruit and train the workers. Its practitioners may be systems designers or managers but they are increasingly likely to be working in large project-based teams that include technicians, trainers, human resources managers, managers who liaise with customers and suppliers and representatives of the local state, logistics experts, lawyers, and a host of other specialists. Their "soft" and "knowledge-based" skills are not just used to develop new systems and refine and troubleshoot older ones; they are also essential for the management of these systems once they are up and running, including "knowledge management."

This schematic overview demonstrates that creative work is involved in a range of different activities that are crucial to the development of capitalism. However, it warns us against any assumption that the relationship between a worker's creativity and the capitalist employer takes a single standard form. Rather, creative labor should be conceived as something extremely heterogeneous that is, moreover, undergoing rapid and dynamic change. This overview also demonstrates the impossibility of distinguishing "creative work" in any definitive way from other forms of work that can be loosely described as "knowledge work." Nevertheless, creative work can, perhaps, be said to have some distinguishing features that are worth investigating further. I now address these.

WHAT IS DISTINCTIVE ABOUT CREATIVE WORK?

As already noted, it is impossible to draw an absolute line between creative work and other forms of knowledge work in any structural analysis that looks at its relation to capital. Nevertheless, if we change the focus to the agency of creative workers and the ways in which their occupational identities have been socially and historically shaped, it becomes possible to identify some features, which, though neither unique to these creative workers nor universally prevalent among them, could be said to characterize them in certain distinctive ways. They are of interest here because they may be hypothesized to shape these workers' attitudes to their work and their relationships with employers and clients.

One of these features is a high commitment to the work itself. Applying one's mind to solving a new problem, as opposed to repeating a known activity, is of the essence in creative work, a process that Karl Marx in the *Grundrisse* described in these terms:

> This overcoming of obstacles is in itself a liberating activity—and further, the external aims become stripped of the semblance of merely external natural urgencies, and become posited as aims which the individual himself posits—hence as self-realization, objectification of the subject, hence real freedom, whose action is, precisely, labor.[14]

Even if, much of the time, creative workers are engaged in mundane or repetitive work that does not require such original mental effort, insofar as this sort of problem-solving is involved, there is a sense in which this work contains elements of "really free labor" that is experienced as unalienated—a form of personal fulfillment.[15] This constitutes a source of genuine satisfaction, creating an additional motive to work that cannot be subsumed into the simple economic motive of earning a living. The worker does not only care about the monetary reward but also about the work's content (or intellectual property), which, even after it has been sold, may still be experienced as in some sense "owned"—something of which it is possible to be proud. This attachment to the work may express itself in the form of a commitment to service users (for instance in education), audiences (for instance in performing arts), or customers (for instance in product design). It may also be linked with concerns about the worker's own personal reputation. In any bargaining process with employers or clients, trade-offs may be made between financial reward and other factors, such as public acknowledgment, a prestigious client, or a greater degree of artistic freedom. This makes for a form of negotiation that is complicated in comparison with other employment relationships, and may be disadvantageous to the worker financially, especially in a situation with an oversupply of creative labor.

This strong identification with the product of the labor can leave workers with an illusion of continuing ownership, even when their intellectual property rights and control have been handed over. Being faced with the reality of this loss may then be painful. The experience of expropriation may come as a recurring shock, closer to the surface of consciousness than in other forms of work where alienation is taken for granted. To the extent that it is genuinely innovative, creative work could be said to be permanently poised at the moment of alienation, and the creative worker repeatedly present at the center of a contradictory drama of expropriation: the work, as it comes into being, both belongs to and is torn away from its begetter. Part of this belonging is the risk of failure; no innovation can be known before it comes into being (if it did, it would not be an innovation), so each time there is a risk that it will not work, or will be found ugly or otherwise unacceptable. Because in that moment of creativity the worker has not yet separated from his/her creation, such failures may be experienced as the results of personal inadequacy. The potential for rejection lurks always in the background of the creation-expropriation drama. This is most obviously acute in forms of creative work that are overtly affective and demand self-exposure (for example, the performing arts, fiction-writing, or film direction), but it hovers less visibly over many other kinds.

The identification of creative workers with their output was illustrated in the WORKS Project by several fashion designers. One said, "For me, fashion is a continuation of myself."[16] Two other designers were even more graphic: "When you're a designer, it gets you in the guts," said one, and another: "It's a job you have to love because we spill our guts out."[17]

But performers and designers are not the only creative workers who make themselves vulnerable in carrying out their work, as is evidenced in the ubiquity of statements like "You're only as good as your last project" or "I put my reputation on the line."

The personal identification of the innovative worker with his or her innovative idea also gives rise to another set of contradictions: between the individual and the collective interest, and between competition and collaboration. If your ideas and knowledge are all you have to sell in the labor market, then they constitute a precious personal asset that, for reasons of self-interest, should not be parted with freely but should be guarded and kept for future sale wherever possible. Offering these to the employer or sharing them with colleagues, with little guarantee of reward, can seem like a form of generosity verging on career suicide. However, few forms of creative work can be carried out in isolation. Most involve teamwork and, for the team to be successful, there is an equally strong self-interested imperative to share knowledge. A general willingness to share enables both learning and teaching; it also improves the overall standard of the project as a whole, thus enhancing everyone's chances of further work. This may also be linked for creative workers to a craving for recognition. Ideas may be shared, even with competitors, for the reward of appreciation or admiration, thus exacerbating still further the tension between wanting to share and wanting to hoard.

Another associated feature of many types of creative work is that it has a "meaning" in the form of some sort of ideological content or potential for social impact, positive or negative. Creative workers therefore have ethical choices to make about how their work is carried out. Sometimes this is linked to a formal responsibility, for instance, in rules of professional conduct or in codes of practice. In other cases, it is up to individual workers to make a personal judgment about where to draw the line between meeting the demands of the employer or client on the one hand and standing by their own values on the other. Where creative workers feel themselves to have responsibility without power, taking an ethical stand may entail considerable courage and sacrifice. Failure to do so may result in being haunted by guilt.

We can conclude that although creative workers form part of a continuum with other workers whose work, albeit knowledge-based, would not normally be regarded as creative, their experiences exhibit in a particular acute form a range of contradictions that, in more routine occupations, lie deeper below the surface. To the extent that they are actively engaged with a quest for meaning in their work, feel personally attached to it, seek aesthetic or moral rewards from it, and invest their powers of mental focus on addressing the challenges it poses to them, they are unable to engage in the simple form of economic transaction that forms the basis of a labor market—"How much will you pay for my bodily time and effort?"—without additional qualification and trade-off. This would seem to create a marketplace in which capital holds most of the bargaining power. However, creative workers also hold some strong cards: they are not, as are many other workers, interchangeable with anyone else with equal bodily strength, endurance, and agility; they have something capital desperately needs in order to develop further—new and original ideas. But, in a rapidly changing economy, these ideas have a short shelf-life, and, with employers able to tap into an expanding global creative workforce, the competition is fierce. It is therefore not easy to predict how creative workers will fare in the next phase of capital restructuring. To set the context, the next section summarizes current trends in the restructuring of knowledge-based work.

CURRENT TRENDS IN THE RESTRUCTURING OF KNOWLEDGE-BASED WORK

The WORKS Project carried out its research in a range of different industries in contrasting national settings and interviewed large numbers of workers in occupational groups ranging from forklift operators to senior scientists in cutting-edge R&D laboratories. Nevertheless, despite numerous national, sectoral, and occupational differences, it uncovered some strong common trends linked to value chain restructuring. One of the most noticeable of these is a general trend of work *intensification*, which is

> not only a lengthening of working hours, but also as a saturation of time, a speeding up of pace and rhythm, tighter deadlines, higher pressure, and sometimes a "colonization" of the other spheres of the individual's life.[18]

In some cases, this is experienced as continuous round-the-clock pressure. In other cases, intensification takes the form of expecting workers to add new tasks to their existing core activities, a concept that can be regarded as "skill intensification," as opposed to a simple upskilling.

> First, the new competencies required from occupational groups involved in restructuring are not necessarily related to the core of their profession, but rather seem to concern "side" skills such as social skills, problem-solving skills and resource management skills. Hence, these new competencies come on top of the existing professional requirements and may even push aside the further development of the core professional skills. Second, "upskilling" is often related to a considerable work intensification and an enlargement of the skills that the employees need: . . . to understand and combine very different types of knowledge and the required speed to process and apply a lot of information in a short time.[19]

Work intensification is particularly noticeable in project-based work. In R&D,[20] for instance, there has been a sharp increase in orientation toward markets, with "pure" research increasingly being ousted by research that can be readily brought to market, exposing workers to direct pressures from the market, experienced as tight deadlines. In general, the regulation of work has increasingly shifted from one based on working time to one based on "work done."

Linked to this intensification of work is a general *speed-up* of its pace. Sometimes this is the result of a general drive to improve efficiency or competitiveness, but often it is a response to market pressure. In the fashion industry, for instance, "the most conspicuous feature is the overall acceleration of business activities and workflows. Across the industry, the traditional pattern of seasonal collections has dissolved, and collections are continuously modified and updated . . . retailers and distributors demand increasingly rapid responses."[21]

This is exacerbated by the global division of labor in the industry. The longer it takes for finished products to be transported (for instance, by boat from Asia) the less time is available for creative work. As Krings et al,[22] put it: "The consequence of this development is a dramatic reduction of the time required for production and of the time available for inspiration, creation and innovation."

> According to the interviewees,[23] time pressure leads to an impoverishment of creativity for designers. Moreover, checking and improving stages of design are shorter and shorter, and sometimes simply removed, leading to more stress. . . . It can also lead to dissatisfaction related to a loss of control over the results of their own work, particularly because the results of their work play a crucial role in their self-fulfillment and are essential for the expression of their own subjectivity.[24]

A third striking transversal trend is that of *standardization*. In R&D, for instance, there is:

> a growing formalization and standardization of the tasks in view of facilitating communication along the value chain. However, this does not mean that tasks are necessarily becoming simpler. The use of project management tools and more documentation of the work are examples of such formalization that originally applied to market-related and commissioned research projects but are then increasingly transferred to all the work of the unit.[25]

Many of the software development professionals perceived standardization as a threat to their own expertise: as their expertise becomes more easily transferred or shared, specialists become more interchangeable.[26]

The fashion designers who were interviewed also complained of the ways in which trends toward standardization were reducing their scope for creativity. In some cases this was linked to the increasing requirement to use image-processing software packages and to make use of standardized component modules. One German designer described how the modular construction system they were forced to use meant that pockets always had to be the same standard shape, "and that's something that we designers do very, very reluctantly" A French designer spoke of the work becoming "industrial" and losing its creativity.[27]

Standardization is a prerequisite for outsourcing and relocation, but once it has taken place it can also make it easier for further outsourcing and relocation to take place in a recursive process that can be described as a "snowball effect."[28] However, managers often underestimate the amount of tacit knowledge required to enable supposedly standardized systems to operate smoothly. In order to get the job done, workers have to bring into play creativity, skills, and knowledge for which they are not credited or rewarded. This sometimes results in an unseen slippage of tasks from knowledge workers to others further down the chain.[29]

Intensification, speed-up, and standardization of work are three of the most universal trends accompanying global value chain restructuring. Many other trends affect knowledge-intensive work, some of which are more specific to particular industries or occupational groups. These include: an increasing requirement to work in response to customer demands, whether these are embodied in contracts or more ad hoc, and to absorb the impact of customer dissatisfaction; an increasing requirement to be available round-the-clock, to communicate with workers or clients in other time zones, and to use global languages (especially English); a need to exercise communications and emotional skills on top of their "core" expertise; an increased likelihood of having to work to targets or performance indicators; the introduction of new forms of monitoring and control; pooling of specialist knowledge into broader databases, leading to the development of two-tier structures with a small number of specialists and a larger number of increasingly interchangeable generic workers; bundling of services into standardized marketable products; externalization of labor to service users, for instance via self-service websites; and a general casualization of employment relationships with a "just-in-time" approach to staffing that puts the entire workforce under continual stress.[30]

CONTROL AND AUTONOMY IN CREATIVE WORK

As already noted, in contemporary capitalism there is no single standard form of relationship between creative workers and those who pay for their work. They may be paid a salary, a fee, a commission, a royalty, or a lump sum for what they produce. They may be employees, independent entrepreneurs, freelancers, partners, franchisers, or day laborers. Just as there are multiple forms of contractual relationship, there are also multiple forms of control. And, to make things even more complicated, these forms of control are not necessarily single or stable; several may coexist alongside each other, and one may transmute into another. Global value chain restructuring often involves changing patterns of overall governance and, within these, shifting power relationships among different units along the chain. The impact of the changing relationships of control between these units is experienced on particular sites as a change in the style of management and the degree of coercion exerted by managers over the local workforce.[31]

As Amanda Damarin has observed, "There is no clear consensus on how control operates or what autonomy looks like in post-industrial settings."[32] Empirical observation throws up a number of distinctive types, each of which is modified by contextual factors including national culture and tradition, gender relations, and factors specific to a particular firm or sector.

One of these types is *personal* control exercised through relationships and obligations between known individuals. This could be a paternalistic form of control exercised through family relationships, for instance in the setting of a family firm, or it could be a more individual form of patronage like that of an aristocrat for a favorite artist. It might be thought that such forms of control are increasingly anachronistic, edged out on the one hand by equal opportunity recruitment and promotion policies and on the other by the impersonal nature of the standardized procedures adopted by global companies for quality-control purposes as well as by public bodies for bureaucratic reasons. Caricatured in the Hollywood "casting couch" stereotype, this form of control has been associated for many years with the entertainment industry. The increasing precariousness of labor markets in these and other "creative" industries means that it still thrives, encouraged by such practices as the provision of work experience through unpaid internships to keen young creative hopefuls. This form of control is bolstered by gift relationships, the mutual exchange of "favors," and complicity in ignoring the formal terms of contracts. It can not only lead subordinated creative workers into situations that are highly exploitative but can also make it impossible to seek recourse if the relationship breaks down. It may also be associated with forms of sexual predation or harassment. The forms of resistance to this type of control open to workers are individual and informal: outmaneuvering the boss, using personal charm or manipulation, using gossip networks to shame and blame, or simply walking away.

A second type of control is *bureaucratic.* This form is exercised through formal and explicit rules, often negotiated with trade unions. It has traditionally been the dominant form not only in the public sector but also in other large organizations, such as banks. It is associated with hierarchical structures and strict rules of entry, with many of the characteristics of an "internal labor market."[33] Here the forms of resistance open to workers include subverting the rules, operating them obstructively or obeying them only minimally (as in the form of trade union action known as "working to rule"), or formally challenging them in order to negotiate improvements in workers' interests, for instance by reducing agreed working hours, increasing rewards, lengthening rest breaks, etc.

A third type is the sort of *Tayloristic* control anatomized by Braverman.[34] In essence, this involves a system of management (and sometimes also of payment) by results. Targets or quotas may be set individually or for a whole team. In the latter case, simple instrumental rationality is not the only motive to work: workers' solidarity with teammates is leveraged as an additional form of motivation. Control may be exerted overtly by a line manager. Or, more insidiously, as Michael Burawoy observed, it may be internalized and become a form of self-exploitation by complicit workers.[35] In an era when targets may be set by external agents—for instance the client company for outsourced services or embedded in quality standards or the design of software systems, when much work can be monitored electronically, and when teams are provisional and geographically distributed, Tayloristic systems of control may be hard to pin down, with a high degree of internalization of control by workers and with the source of power often invisible. The most effective form of resistance to Taylorism takes place prior to its introduction, and involves resistance to standardization, demands for more varied work, job rotation, or the introduction of various forms of job enrichment or "human-centered design."[36] These have rarely been achieved outside Scandinavia. Once it has been introduced, apart from out-and-out sabotage, forms of resistance to Tayloristic management include conscious collective efforts by groups of workers to slow down the pace of work in order to gain some time and reduce stress,[37] negotiations over the type and level of targets or performance indicators, and the use of health and safety regulations to try to ensure that stress and speed-up do not reach inhuman levels. Many of these are difficult for creative workers to adopt, because they imply an attitude that inhibits creativity. An interesting case here is that of the California employees of the video game company Electronic Arts, who, despite the fact that their work involved producing the audio and video content for the company's games, had to prove that their work was *not* "creative" in order to win a class action suit against their employer to gain a reduction in working hours.[38]

A fourth type is control by the *market.* Unless what they have to offer is exceptionally sought-after, self-employed workers and independent producers have little choice but to offer what their customers want, at the price they are prepared to pay, in the face of competition that, in many industries, is increasingly global. Although there may be some scope for individual negotiation in some circumstances, the main form of resistance here lies in the creation of professional associations, guilds, or trade unions in which suppliers combine in order to try to set out basic ground rules and avoid undercutting one another. Actors, writers, and photographers are examples of groups that have achieved this, to some extent. However, in any such grouping there is always a tension between competition and collaboration: between the urge to become a star no matter what the cost and the compensations of solidarity. Insofar as it is successful, this kind of resistance strategy can lead to another form of control, exercised through the membership of the association, which might be called *peer* or *professional* control. In some cases, self-regulating professional bodies, such as those that represent lawyers and doctors, have succeeded in institutionalizing such forms of control with sufficient success to enable them to become embedded in national or even international regulations. With forceful sanctions, including the right to exclude transgressing members from practicing their professions, many such organizations exert considerable power. Even these, however, are currently under threat of modification, if not erosion, from the commodification of knowledge.[39]

Damarin[40] argues that within particular industries (her own case study concerned Web designers) other, more diffused forms of control exist, which she refers to as "socio-technical networks consisting of relationships to persons, technologies, conventions, and typifications." This conception has some features in common with the concept of "communities of practice."[41] Rather than seeing this as a separate form of control, I prefer to regard it as a striking and insightful characterization of the complexity of control patterns in creative work in which elements of several of the various forms of control discussed above (and others I have not mentioned) may be brought together in particular configurations in specific regional, cultural, and industrial contexts.

The management of creative workers is widely recognized as a challenge for capital. A recent article in *The Economist* put it like this:

> Managing creativity involves a series of difficult balancing acts: giving people the freedom to come up with new ideas but making sure that they operate within an overall structure, creating a powerful corporate culture but making sure that it is not too stifling.[42]

In practice, this may often mean the coexistence of more than one form of control, involving both sticks and carrots. But, as we have noted, each form of control evokes a different form of resistance. A defensive response appropriate to one form of management aggression may be futile or even counterproductive if it is adopted in relation to another. For instance, in a situation in which workers are obliged to work excessively long hours, invoking an official regulation that limits the working week (an appropriate response in a situation of bureaucratic control) will have little effect if workers are paid only if they meet certain targets (a Tayloristic form of control) or if they believe that they will bring disgrace on their family firm if they leave a job unfinished (a personal form of control) or if they know that their reputation depends on completing it on time (a market form of control).

When several forms of control exist alongside each other, the contradictory pressures on workers seem to be so great that they are often disempowered from adopting any effective form of resistance. Instead, they may only be able to respond by becoming physically or mentally ill, letting their families take the strain (or abstaining from any form of adult family life altogether),[43] burning out, dropping out, striking a pose of cynical anomie, indulging in isolated acts of "letting off steam" or sabotage, or adopting a ruthless "devil take the hindmost" attitude that may involve trampling on the interests of fellow workers. Developing new forms of collective organization and resistance is, of course, an alternative option but one that we found rather little evidence for in the WORKS research.[44]

Case study research throws up many examples of such contradictions. For instance, as already noted, the standardization and fragmentation, or "modularization,"[45] of tasks and processes that is a requisite for outsourcing or relocating them requires Tayloristic forms of management. However, in order for these fragmented labor processes to be managed seamlessly over time and space and across cultural divides new "soft" skills are also required that require commitment and motivation and cannot be managed Tayloristically.

In discussing the WORKS results, Ramioul and De Vroom speak of the "prisoner's dilemma" of knowledge sharing in software production. On the one hand, companies midway down the chain want to outsource as many activities as possible to cheaper locations in order to keep their costs down and remain competitive.

On the other, they are well aware that their supplier companies, further down, want to "move up the chain" to get higher value contracts. Two companies may thus become clamped together in a relationship that is both strongly mutually dependent and intensely competitive (if company A passes on too much knowledge to company B it may find itself outbid and bypassed altogether when the contract comes up for renewal).[46] Similar dilemmas can arise when individuals are thrust temporarily together in a team: on this project, they need each other's trust and collaboration; on the next, they may be locked in deadly competition.

Premilla D'Cruz and Ernesto Noronha describe a case in an Indian call center where the very tight targets are set by client organizations in Service Level Agreements (SLAs).[47] Local management, though exerting such strict control that the authors regard it as "depersonalized bullying," nevertheless manage to escape the consequences of this, at least in the form of any direct resistance by the workforce. By blaming the external clients, appealing to their workers' loyalty to the national back office processing (BPO) industry, and inculcating an idea of call center staff as "professionals," these managers have succeeded in demonizing trade unions, deflecting direct hostility to themselves, and persuading the workforce to internalize many of the control mechanisms that push them to reach their targets. The buildup of pressure, however, is so extreme that the workers have to resort to occasional acts of sabotage as a way of "letting off steam."

Another case study illustrates the contradictions that arise when restructuring substitutes one type of management for another. One study examined a reorganization of the Danish tax system, whereby a number of specialized professional tax experts, who had previously been employed by different national and local government departments under civil-service-type forms of management, were transformed into a large centralized pool of more or less generic tax advisors giving information to the public by telephone and email in a call-center organizational model. Although softened by the context, which was one of active collaboration between the trade union and the management to ensure a transition that did not do too much violence to their professional norms, this was essentially a substitution of a Tayloristic form of management for a bureaucratic one. Collectively, these workers, who typically had a long-term loyalty to their employers, had built up a large body of knowledge (sometimes in part tacit) over many years. Pooling this knowledge in shared databases and introducing Tayloristic forms of control appeared to be quite successful in the short term. However, it raised big questions about how the knowledge could be updated in the future. With all their working time spent either in meetings or on the phone to customers, staff did not have a chance to update their knowledge; and the higher staff turnover and flexible work practices associated with the new form of organization meant that new recruits were much less knowledgeable than the workers they replaced. Short-term gains for the organization could lead to serious problems in the future.[48]

Such examples could be multiplied. I hope I have presented enough evidence to demonstrate that the interaction between different management drives for control does not only create near-paralyzing contradictions for creative workers, but also creates contradictions for management itself.

CONCLUSIONS

We can conclude that, for capital, there is a contradiction between, on the one hand, the need for a continuous (but dispensable) supply of new ideas and talent in order to fuel its accumulation process and, on the other, the need to control these processes tightly in order to maximize efficiency and profit and to appropriate the intellectual property so that companies are able to trade freely in the resulting commodities. On the side of labor, there is the urge by individual workers to do something meaningful in life, make a mark on the world, be recognized and appreciated and respected, on the one hand, and, on the other, the need for a subsistence income, the ability to plan ahead, and some spare time to spend with loved ones. This is often expressed as a contradiction between a drive for autonomy and a search for security. These contradictions are played out against each other in a complex dance in which different forms of managerial control give rise to (or bypass) different forms of resistance by workers. New twists in the organization of global value chains are constantly confronting workers with new shocks and surprises, even—or perhaps especially—those who have in the past regarded themselves as skilled and specialist enough to have a strong bargaining position. Meanwhile, unexpected new ideas from labor could pose new risks to management. (Who, twenty years ago, could have predicted the ways in which Indian software engineers are able to use the Internet to inform themselves of global rates of pay for the work they are doing and use this to their advantage in the global labor market?)

With multiple forms of employment relationship and multiple types of relationship to intellectual property there is no single, simple way to characterize the relationship between creative labor and capital. This very heterogeneity, and the many contradictions it gives rise to, could, however, constitute as much of a strength as a weakness—to either side. Perhaps it is time for creative workers to invest some of their creativity in finding ways to exploit these contradictions.

6. Crisis as Capitalist Opportunity

The New Accumulation through Public Service Commodification

The year 2008 marked a turning point for international capital, with the financial crisis providing an unprecedented opportunity to embark on a new phase of accumulation based not on what might be called "primary primitive accumulation" (the generation of new commodities from natural resources or activities carried out outside the money economy) but on the commodification of public services. In this commodification process, which might be regarded as a kind of "secondary primitive accumulation," activities already carried out in the paid economy for their use value (such as education, or health care) are standardized in such a way that they can be traded for profit and appropriated by capital: use value is thereby transformed into exchange value.[1] This secondary form of accumulation is based on the expropriation, not of nature or unalienated aspects of life, nor of unpaid domestic labor, but of the results of past struggles by workers for the redistribution of surplus value in the form of universal public services. It thus constitutes a *re*appropriation and as such its impacts on working-class life are multiple and pernicious.

For the workers actually delivering public services, new forms of alienation are introduced when these services are commodified and there is generally a deterioration in working conditions. However, there are also larger implications for workers in other sectors, because public sector workers are, in most developed countries, the last remaining bastion of trade union strength and decent working conditions, setting the standards for other workers to aspire to. This means that the erosion of the bargaining position of public sector workers also represents a defeat for all workers in their capacities *as* workers. At an even more general level, past gains are snatched from the working class as a whole (including children, the elderly, the sick, and the unemployed). This last effect cannot, of course, remain invisible and understandably becomes a focus of opposition. However, a political strategy based only on "fighting the cuts" risks giving the impression that it is simply the scale of state expenditure that is in contest, rendering invisible the underlying logic of commodification and the new reality that public services themselves have become a site of accumulation that is crucial for the continuing expansion of international capital. The new reality is one in which large sections of capital actually have a vested interest in an *enlarged* public service sector, but one in which services are standardized and capable of being delivered by a compliant and interchangeable workforce, embedded in a global division of labor, and subjected to the discipline of that global labor market. This raises new contradictions for the relationship between the state and capital.

It is increasingly difficult, if not impossible, to separate "finance capital" from "productive capital" either analytically or empirically.[2] I will not attempt here to disentangle the complex interactions between the lead-up to the 2008 financial crisis and the restructuring of transnational organizations, or the ways in which the holding companies that own supposedly non-financial organizations are increasingly behaving like financial ones. Nevertheless, in order to understand this phenomenon, it is necessary to outline some of the background conditions that have led to the emergence of the new breed of multinational corporations currently waxing fat on the commodification of public services.

The 2008 financial crisis coincided with a crisis of profitability for international capital that was already undergoing massive restructuring. One aspect of this restructuring was a huge growth in the concentration of capital. The year 2007 represented a peak in global investment flows, with global FDI flows reaching their highest level ever ($1.833 trillion), surpassing the 2000 peak.[3] There was also a record level of cross-border mergers and acquisitions, with the number rising by 12 percent and the value (some $1.637 trillion) up 21 percent on the previous year.[4] UNCTAD estimated that the total sales of 79,000 transnational corporations (TNCs) and their 790,000 foreign affiliates amounted in that year to $31 trillion—a 21 percent increase over 2006—while the total number of their employees rose to some 82 million. The 100 largest TNCs, in particular, strengthened their global grip, with combined foreign assets estimated at $570 billion.[5] However, despite this huge growth, the number of green-field FDI projects actually *decreased*—from 12,441 in 2006 to 11,703 in 2007.[6] This indicates that though the process of concentration was accelerating, there was actually a slowdown in the generation of new production. In other words, the largest TNCs were sustaining their profits not so much as a result of new production but through the cannibalization of preexisting production capacity. Without some new source of commodities from which to generate surplus value, the preconditions were in place for a decline in profitability. When few parts of the world were left outside the scope of global capitalism, where might these new commodities be found?

Associated with this trend was a major reorganization of value chains. Facilitated by a combination of neoliberal trade policies and the widespread introduction of the information and communications technologies that make it easy to relocate economic activities and manage them remotely, the previous decade had seen an acceleration of the trend to modularize business processes in such a way that they could be reconfigured in a variety of different contractual and spatial permutations and combinations. In the late 1990s, "offshore outsourcing" still seemed something of a risky experiment.[7] A decade later it had come to seem such a normal part of business-as-usual that U.S. and European managers were expected to justify why they had *not* opened call centers in India, shared service centers in Russia, or design studios in Vietnam, alongside their production facilities in China. Most large corporations had systematically anatomized their business processes, broken them down into standardized units, and, unit by unit, decided whether to concentrate them on a single site or distribute them around the world, whether to keep them in-house or outsource them, and whether to search for the lowest price or the highest quality or some combination of these things. In aggregate, these decisions had brought about major upheavals. By 2008 a new global division of labor had emerged,[8] with new patterns of regional specialization and new corporate and sectoral configurations. As more and more economic activities became tradable, large companies embarked upon a dual process of disaggregation and aggregation, shuffling and reshuffling these activities into new combinations.[9] While some companies continued to focus on their traditional strengths in manufacturing or the extraction of natural resources, others consolidated their positions as suppliers of services. By 2006, one in five (20 percent) of the 100 largest non-financial TNCs listed by UNCTAD was a company providing services, compared with only 7 percent in 1997.

As these huge service companies expanded their markets, the services they supplied became more generic, increasingly developing the character of standard commodities, so standardized that, in many cases, it was possible to supply essentially the same services (for instance, IT services, payroll administration, or customer services) to client companies regardless of which economic sector they were in: manufacturing, retail, utilities, or other sectors. Most of their customer companies were no longer operating in a buyer's market acquiring bespoke services tailored to their individual needs; rather, they were becoming like shoppers in a chain store, selecting from among a range of standard models offered by the seller. Once such a supply reaches critical mass, a harsh economic logic sets in: the larger the market for these services is, and the more that standardization can be achieved, then the lower the price will become. Soon, even customers whose preference might be to continue to produce these services for themselves in-house, or to buy them tailor-made from a small local supplier, are driven by the relentless logic of the market (in which the relative cost of customization has become exorbitantly expensive compared with the purchase of standard products) to realize that such personalization is a luxury, and to follow the crowd to the cheapest supplier. In IT-based business services, in particular, this logic has been given an extra push through the dominance of standard software packages (such as those supplied by Microsoft) or platforms (such as those supplied by SAP Business Management Systems) and the ways that these may be bundled in with the services supplied by global suppliers of telecommunications, energy, or other infrastructure services. However, IT-enabled industries are by no means the only examples of sellers' markets in the supply of services; large multinational corporations are also increasingly involved in supplying manual labor, either through labor-only subcontracting by temporary employment agencies or through the outsourced provision of security, care, cleaning or other services. Increasingly prominent among the customers of these service companies, over the past decade, have been public sector organizations.

In the early years of the twenty-first century, these trends reinforced one another, producing a situation whereby large service supply companies (with their own internal global divisions of labor) were desperate to expand. With limited opportunities to grow through acquisition and merger, and markets in many other sectors nearing saturation, the public sector offered a tempting new field for expansion. By 2008, according to a report published by the UK government, outsourced public services accounted for nearly 6 percent of GDP in the UK, directly employing over

1.2 million people, with a turnover of £79 billion in 2007–8—an increase of 126 percent over the estimated £31 billion in 1995–6. The report dubbed this rapidly-expanding sector the public services industry (PSI) and noted that, in terms of value added, it "is significantly larger than 'food, beverages and tobacco' (23bn in 2006), 'communications' (£28bn), 'electricity, gas and water supply' (£32bn) and 'hotels and catering' (£36bn)." This phenomenon is not peculiar to Britain. As a share of GDP, the PSI sector was estimated in that year to be even higher in Sweden and Australia. In absolute terms, the UK PSI market, at £79.4 billion, was second only to that of the United States (at £393bn), but the sector was nevertheless significant in scale elsewhere, with an estimated value, for instance, of £44.8 billion in France, £32.2 billion in Australia, and £24.7 billion in Spain. If a somewhat broader definition were to be applied, encompassing former public utilities like post, telecommunications, water, and energy, these figures would be considerably larger.[10]

Large though these sums are, they represent only a fraction of the total value of public services. Despite the neoliberal anti–big-government-rhetoric of the last quarter-century, despite the very real cutbacks in services that have been experienced by working people as a withdrawal of state support, and despite the sale of public assets,[11] government spending has risen inexorably in all OECD countries both in absolute terms and as a percentage of GDP. Whereas in 1960, government spending was an average 28.4 percent of GDP across the OECD, by 1980 this had risen to 43.8 percent, and since continued to creep up to reach 47.7 percent in 2009. This varies somewhat by country, with Japan, at 39.7 percent, the United States at 42.2 percent, and Canada, at 43.8 percent, relatively near the bottom of the range, and the Netherlands, Sweden, France, Austria, Belgium, and Italy near the top, each with government spending between 50 percent and 54 percent of GDP. The UK and Germany are close to the average, at 47.2 percent and 47.6 percent respectively.[12] An analysis based on government spending per person produces a different ranking, with the United States (in which total government spending is estimated at nearly $6 trillion) above Italy, Canada, Britain, and Japan, partly because of its much higher military spending.[13] However the figures are broken down, this represents a potential field for expansion that is staggering in its scale, a market that, ironically enough, with the notable exception of the militarized United States, is proportionally largest in precisely those countries that, as a result of democratic pressure from below, have built the most comprehensive welfare states. This is how social-democrat Sweden, regarded by Gøsta Esping-Anderson[14] and others as having achieved the highest degree of decommodification of any developed capitalist economy, contrived to top the list of countries with the largest share of outsourced government services in 2008: the more decommodification, the more scope for recommodification.

HOW HAS THIS MARKET been levered open? Procurement of services from external providers is not new, of course. For centuries governments have commissioned buildings, roads, bridges, and other "public works," and purchased goods, ranging from paperclips to fire engines, from private suppliers. And for just as long there have been scandals relating to the greasing of public servants' palms by suppliers to acquire these lucrative contracts. However, it is probably most useful to date the origins of the current wave of outsourcing to the early 1980s. In the UK, the Conservative government pioneered two distinctively different forms of privatization. One of these was the direct sale of public assets, originally promoted as sales to individual citizens rather than to companies. The most high-profile of these were the sales of council houses to their tenants and, starting in 1984, of public utilities—telecommunications, gas, and electricity—via widely publicized share issues, which the general public were invited to buy. Associated with the latter, though less well publicized, was the opening up of telecommunications and energy markets to competition from private companies. The other form of privatization (not involving a total change of ownership) was the government-enforced introduction of "compulsory competitive tendering," first into local government and then into the National Health Service (NHS). Though this did not necessarily mean that the services in question *had* to be carried out by external contractors, in-house departments, employing public servants, were now obliged to compete with private companies to be able to continue providing the service in question. This brought downward pressure on wages and conditions and introduced a new precariousness: jobs were no longer necessarily "for life" but only guaranteed for the duration of the contract.

This first swathe of competitive tendering involved mainly manual tasks such as construction work, waste disposal, and cleaning, perhaps not coincidentally also the areas where public sector unions were strong, and had demonstrated this strength in the widespread strikes of the "winter of discontent" of 1978–79 that directly preceded Thatcher's election victory. Much of the rhetoric surrounding this enforced outsourcing centered not just on the supposed efficiencies that would be gained through the delivery of services by private companies, unconstrained by the "restrictive practices" of public sector manual unions, but on a discourse of "enterprise": the external provision of these services, it was claimed, would create openings for new small firms. In reality, the majority of the contracts went to large, often multinational companies. In 1984–85, for example, while public attention was focused on the national strike by coal miners—the other group of organized workers directly targeted by Thatcher's Tories—another long-running strike was taking place at Barking Hospital in East London. The striking cleaners at this hospital were employed by a subsidiary of the Pritchards Services Group, a transnational corporation with fifty-eight subsidiaries in fifteen countries, employing 17,000 people in 430 hospitals worldwide, including Saudi Arabia, South Africa, New Zealand, France, Germany, and the United States.[15] Interestingly, from 1983 to 1994,Thatcher's husband, Denis, was vice-chairman of Attwoods plc, a large international waste management company that stood to gain from precisely this form of privatization.

Each of these forms of privatization had parallels elsewhere. In Europe, Britain played an important role in pushing through a liberalization agenda that first led to the compulsory selling off of national telecommunications providers, then of publicly owned energy companies and the opening up of postal services to the market. There had been EU regulation of public procurement since 1966 (in Directive 66/683, which prohibited rules favoring national suppliers over foreign ones within the single European Market). The turn to neoliberalism brought much broader deregulation in the mid-1980s. The Single European Act of 1986 introduced a new regime in which open tendering procedures were established as the norm for all public supplies in the EU and negotiated procedures were allowed only in exceptional circumstances. The first Utilities Directive (90/351) removed market access barriers to energy, telecommunications, and water, and in 1992 the Services Directive (92/50) extended the principles that had governed the procurement of goods, works, and public utilities to public services more generally.[16]

Meanwhile, the Uruguay Round of the GATT, which commenced in 1986 and culminated in GATT 1994, brought services (along with capital and intellectual property) within the scope of global trade agreements. In 1992, the year in which the International Telecommunications Union (ITU) was established, an era of global telecommunications deregulation opened up the enabling infrastructure for cheap global transfer of digitized information. This was also the year in which India was able to start exporting its software services freely, through the removal of export barriers that had originally been designed to protect an indigenous industry as part of an import-substitution strategy. In the early 1990s, the stage was therefore set for global companies to provide a range of services across national borders, bulldozing their way through any restrictions that might have been set up to protect national companies or local workforces.[17]

These developments coincided historically with the formal ending of the Cold War after 1989. Not only did this open up the countries of the former Soviet Bloc as new markets for Western capital, it also removed any remaining reasons for employers, in collaboration with national governments, to strike the sort of special deals with labor that characterized the third quarter of the twentieth century, variously described as "Fordism," the "golden age," the "postwar Keynesian national welfare state," etc.[18]

THE EROSION OF THESE special deals forms part of the context of the development of the global division of labor practiced by the new business services multinationals. Whether these companies achieve their economies of scale by sending jobs to the places where the skills are abundant and cheap—offshoring—or by bringing cheap labor to the sites where the work is carried out, for instance through the use of migrant workers, they are adopting what is in effect the same strategy: drawing on a global reserve army of labor. Their choices are not, of course, entirely unconstrained. They have to operate within limits set by, for instance, the supply of suitable skills and qualifications, national regulations that restrict the movements of labor, set minimum wages or impose particular quality standards, and the extent to which the existing labor force is able to put up a fight. Nevertheless, insofar as employers can draw on alternative sources of labor, this poses a threat to the wages and conditions of existing workforces and acts as a disciplinary force on them.

The existence of this new global reserve army seems directly associated with the long slow unraveling of labor standards in capitalism's privileged core workforce, with its expectations of job security, promotion, employer-provided pension schemes, paid holidays, sickness compensation, maternity rights, and the other benefits won by workers in the third quarter of the twentieth century. This development cannot, of course, be attributed entirely to the globalization of labor; the direct attacks on organized labor under Thatcher and Reagan, for instance, also clearly played a major role. However, the existence of a global reserve army of labor is certainly a major factor in explaining the failure of workers, even workers who have historically been well organized and highly skilled, to resist the deterioration in their working conditions and wages of the last two decades, a deterioration that is clearly measurable in terms of longer hours, worsening physical and mental health, lower purchasing power of wages, loss of pension coverage, and contractual impermanency. It is hard to escape the conclusion that workers' bargaining position with their employers has been severely undermined by the knowledge that there are other workers out there quite capable of doing their jobs.

It should be noted that in most developed countries up to 2008[19] the major exception to this trend of erosion was among public sector workers. In many countries during the last two decades public sector workers became not just the most strongly unionized part of the workforce[20] but also nearly the only remaining carriers of a set of models of what decent work might look like. Public sector workers have taken the lead in negotiating equal opportunities agreements, trade-offs between time and money that promote a better work–life balance and reinforcing standards that place the quality of service to clients higher than financial considerations.

This is not the place to argue whether a single "Fordist model" of postwar industrial relations can be said to have existed. Whatever particular compromises had been struck between capital and labor in differing national contexts, and whatever the extent to which neoliberal policies had already begun to dismantle them during the 1980s, it can be safely asserted that 1989 marked a moment when the pressures to move toward a convergent global employment model began, almost universally, to exert greater force than any countervailing pressures from labor to protect or extend previous gains.

This process has not been entirely negative for all workers, of course. Because of huge disparities between countries and because of the strongly segmented nature of labor markets, as well as because of the very different degrees with which labor has been able to resist, these leveling processes have represented a relative improvement for some, even as they have been experienced as a deterioration in wages and working conditions by others. In particular, women and people from black and ethnic minorities, part-time and temporary workers, and workers in countries with a history of very poor employment protection benefited, for instance, from various ILO or European directives against discrimination during the 1990s. Nevertheless, an important part of the context of the opening up of public services to the market has been the simultaneous erosion of employment protection and easing of access to a global pool of labor: a reserve army not just of manual workers but also of "information workers," who, thanks to the standardization of white-collar work through the introduction of information and communications technologies, are increasingly able to carry out the tasks that had previously formed part of the job descriptions of civil servants or other public sector bureaucrats. Standardization of tasks and the increasingly generic nature of white-collar labor processes (combined with the ease with which digitized information can be transmitted across distance) have rendered office workers newly substitutable for each other, undermining their bargaining power with employers, whether public or private.

FAR FROM MODIFYING THE more pernicious effects on labor of the marketization of public services of the 1980s and early 1990s, the New Labour government elected to power in the UK in 1997 aggressively pursued further privatization. In local government it replaced what the Conservatives had called "Compulsory Competitive Tendering" with its own "Best Value" initiative, which placed a legal duty on local councils to secure the most economic, efficient and effective services and demonstrate that they had compared all their services with those of other private and public providers. It also introduced a regime of continuous audit and control, reducing the scope for the exercise of individual professionalism and workers' ability to respond directly to the needs of clients. While there was less apparent and immediate legal requirement to outsource, the general legal obligations were broader (and some of the penalties for failing to demonstrate Best Value, just as punitive, if not more so). Perhaps more important, the introduction of this policy involved a change of mindset, with local authorities, of whatever political persuasion, being forced into a process of internalizing the values imposed by the system. Even if services were not outsourced, they had to be managed as if they were, with public servants increasingly placed under the discipline of the market. A precondition for making the required comparisons was that services had to be defined in standardized ways. Best Value can thus be seen as one of the drivers of a process of routinization and standardization of tasks, accompanied by the introduction of performance indicators and protocols, enabling them to be monitored statistically and providing the basis for quality standards to be inscribed in the contracts or Service Level Agreements (SLAs) that define the terms on which private companies provide these formerly public services.

Such New Labour policies thus played a crucial role in the commodification of public services that underpins their transformation into units of exchange in a global market.[21] Local government was not the only target: New Labour also introduced major reforms that developed a market for private companies in the National Health Service,[22] education, prisons, and legal services.[23] In each case, the process of transforming part of a public service into a tradable commodity passed through the same stages: standardization, the creation of demand, persuading the workforce to accept the changes and the transfer of risk.[24] These developments were not, of course, unique to New Labour, or to the UK. However, their enthusiastic endorsement by social democrats in Britain, as in Scandinavia and elsewhere, played an important role in creating a new common sense, whereby it is seen as both natural and inevitable that norms are set by the market.

In the case of complex personal services (such as teaching, nursing, or social work) involving a large body of contextual and tacit knowledge, communication skills and "emotional work,"[25] the standardization processes that underpin commodification are by no means easy to achieve, involving many steps during the course of which tacit knowledge is progressively codified; tasks are standardized; output measures are agreed; management processes are reorganized; organizations are broken down into their constituent parts; the constituent parts are formalized, sometimes as separate legal entities; and market-like relationships are introduced between them. All this may well be preparatory to a change of ownership or opening up a competitive invitation for external subcontractors to take the service over. Only when the activity has been actually or potentially transformed into something that can be made or sold by a profit-making enterprise is the ground prepared for further restructuring in ways that form part of the normal practices of multinational companies: mergers, acquisitions, reconfiguration of parts in new combinations, and the introduction of a global division of labor.[26]

The decade from 1997 to 2007 saw these standardization and internationalization processes proceeding apace. By 2000, an enormous new array of global protocols and quality standards had been put in place, a process that accelerated over the next decade. These include the quality standards set by the International Standardization Organization (ISO).[27] Over 700,000 standards were registered on the ISO's World Standards Service Network (WSSN) database by 2010.[28] In the meantime, skills were also increasingly subject to standardization. Millions of workers around the world gained certificates accredited by Sun, Oracle, Cisco, Microsoft, or other IT companies, enabling them to enter a transparent global job market in such a way that their skills were interchangeable with those of others and clearly understood by employers. It is possible for a newly qualified holder of a Cisco Certificate, for instance, to go to a website[29] and discover that it will earn its holder an average annual salary of US$69,401 in the UK or an average of US$14,518 in India. Those who cannot sell their skills to large multinational corporations, can auction them to the highest bidder on websites like Elance oDesk.[30]To give an indication of the scale of the global reserve army created in this way, it can be noted that just one Microsoft certificate, the Microsoft Certified Professional (MCP), was held at the time of writing by 2,296,561 workers.[31] For an occupation that, as recently as the 1980s, was the preserve of an elite few with considerable bargaining power,[32] this number is staggering.

Many of the companies for whose employ these white-collar workers are competing have grown exponentially over the last quarter-century, sometimes with origins in the service divisions of manufacturing companies but sometimes with roots in financial or business services companies. They include Siemens Business Services, Accenture, Capgemini, and Capita, with a historical base in Europe or North America. But they also include Infosys, Wipro, and Tata Software Consultancy, companies that originated in India, at first providing relatively low-level IT services but soon moving rapidly up the value chain to become global leaders in the supply of offshore business process outsourcing (BPO). There are also companies that focus more on the supply of manual workers, such as Manpower and Group 4 Securicor and companies that specialize in certain sectors or types of service (such as Vertex, which supplies outsourced call center services) as well as others that span many types of activity, such as Serco and ISS.

These companies are not passive players in the global economy. They actively market their services to governments and lobby vigorously for an expansion of outsourcing, either individually or through business associations such as, in the UK, the Business Services Association (BSA) and National Outsourcing Association (NOA). Many have consultancy divisions that advise government bodies on how to "modernize" their services, recommending with one hand the sorts of outsourcing strategies from which they, and other companies, benefit with the other. These consultants are particularly active in emerging markets, such as Vietnam,[33] where the large scale of state services offers rich pickings. Serco has even set up a Serco Institute, which describes itself as "a UK think tank offering research and thought-leadership on the use of competition and contracting in public service reform and the development of sustainable public service markets."[34] Colin Leys and Stewart Player have anatomized the extraordinarily aggressive lobbying of the New Labour and Coalition governments in the UK by global healthcare companies that shaped the 2011 proposals for NHS reform.[35]

Increasingly, the market relationship of such companies with the governments that are their customers is changing from one where the buyers wield the power to a seller's market. One of the factors bringing about this shift of power is the changing nature, and ownership, of the skills and knowledge of the workforce. Traditionally, many public service workers (including teachers, social workers, and health workers) have brought a complex array of skills to their work and have been able to exercise a degree of autonomy in responding individually to their clients. Even in highly bureaucratized rule-driven environments, such as tax offices,[36] workers have possessed a considerable amount of specialist knowledge derived from their experience, much of it not written down. The quality of services has therefore depended crucially on the existence of a stable, committed workforce, often with strongly enforced professional and ethical standards developed within communities of practice with a degree of self-regulation.

The processes that form part of the preconditions for commodification involve an analysis of these skills and the tasks associated with exercising them, breaking them down into their component parts, setting explicit standards for their performance and, often, introducing an elaborated division of labor whereby the more routine tasks are transferred to less-skilled workers. Internalized forms of control exercised by workers themselves and monitored either by their own motivation or through feedback from colleagues or line managers are thus replaced by externally dictated ones. This process takes time, often requiring the gradual handover of work to a new, and differently trained cohort of workers.

It is not only the workforce that has to be retrained, either: service users also have to become accustomed to being treated as consumers in a mass market rather than individual clients. In the early stages of outsourcing, this process is by no means complete. Considerations both of political expediency and of efficiency demand a smooth and seamless transfer, which is experienced by service users as representing in its early stages no deterioration and, if possible, in some respects an improvement, compared with its "wasteful" and "bureaucratic" predecessor. The easiest way to bring about such a transition is to use the same staff to deliver the same service. Thus a typical first outsourcing of any given service (much like a typical corporate takeover) does not involve mass redundancies but rather a transfer of personnel from one employer to another. In Europe, this is eased by TUPE, the EU's Transfer of Undertakings (Protection of Employment) Directive (EC Directive 2001/23). This Directive provides legal protection for transferred employees with respect to their working conditions, including pension entitlements. TUPE's existence has led to a situation in which the trade union reaction to outsourcing is often not to resist it outright but to focus on ensuring that transferred employees are fully covered by the TUPE regulations. Industrial action in public sector outsourcing situations is comparatively rare, though by no means nonexistent.[37] As a result of successive transfers in the locations where outsourcing has first taken place, such as the UK, the skilled workforce of the outsourcing multinationals has expanded not so much through new recruitment in the labor market as through transfers of personnel. In a department providing IT services, for example, or a large outsourced call center, sitting alongside each other, and with very different terms and conditions of employment inherited from their previous employers, workers may be found whose previous employment might have been in a variety of different central or local government departments or in banks, manufacturing companies or service companies. Once employed by the outsourcer, these workers may find that their work undergoes a further series of changes, with some tasks moved to other branches of the company in other regions or countries and, for those remaining, new performance indicators or targets to be met, and new requirements to be available for work at what were formerly regarded as unsocial hours. Since outsourcing contracts are generally of quite a short duration, each contract renewal will involve further restructuring.

In one case study in the UK,[38] a local government IT department was first outsourced to a large European-based global IT firm (Company A). Some employees took redundancy, and others transferred their employment to this company. After a few years, the contract came up for renewal and was won by a smaller, UK-based company (Company B). Some of the originally transferred employees remained in Company A, reabsorbed into different roles, some took redundancy, and some were employed by Company B. Company B was then bought up by a U.S.-based multinational with a strongly anti-union tradition (Company C). The remaining workforce (still providing the same IT service to the same local authority) had thus been employed by four different employers in less than a decade. Although there did not appear to have been any formal breach of TUPE regulations, there had been a steady decline in the quality of working life and in working conditions over this period. One worker, whose child was severely ill with cancer, asked permission of the new management at Company C to work from home a couple of days a week (something that would have been normal under the old local authority collective agreement) and was refused permission by a manager who told him, "If the work can be done from home, it can be done from India."

Even more invidious for many public sector workers than the slow deterioration in working conditions and job security is the shift in values from a public service ethos, in which work is felt to have some intrinsic meaning, to a commercial environment where the work leads only to "filling the pockets of the shareholders," in the words of one IT technician. Many have consciously made a choice to work in the public sector, sacrificing promotion possibilities for what is seen as a secure and rewarding job that makes a contribution to the community.[39] When forcibly transformed into private sector workers, they may become disgruntled employees, refusing to acquire the "lean and mean" attitudes that command respect in the multinational companies for which they now work, but, to the company, this does not much matter. Once their expertise has been acquired by the company, they can be replaced by a younger, more malleable workforce, grateful for whatever security it can get. In the UK, the Labour government did provide some protection for second-generation employees in outsourced public services, with a "two-tier" code on terms and conditions in outsourced services that ensured that new employees working alongside former public sector workers received the same pay and pensions. However, this code was withdrawn in December 2010 by the incoming coalition government.[40] A comparison of working conditions in the same occupations in the public, private and voluntary sectors in the UK, using data from the Labour Force Survey, found that in each case conditions were worse in the private sector. For instance, only 3 percent of prison officers in the public sector had job tenure of less than a year compared with 11 percent of those in the private sector, and 10 percent of full-time health care and personal service workers in the private sector worked more than 48 hours per week compared with only 2 percent in the public sector.[41]

Once the knowledge of former public sector workers has been stripped and coded and placed in standard databases, it can not only be transferred to cheaper employees, it can also be used as an asset by the new employer. For example, a company that has already gained the experience of running a local government helpline, managing the HR system of a university, supplying the IT to run a tax system, or providing the laundry service for a hospital is then able to market this service aggressively to other potential public customers, in other regions or countries. Commodified workers' knowledge thus provides the raw material for capital's expansion.

THERE IS NOW A SUFFICIENT accumulation of commodified workers' knowledge by TNC service provider companies to propel a huge extension in the scope and scale of outsourcing. In the targets of the PSI companies are a wide range of services, with education and health seen as offering the greatest scope for growth.[42] A particularly tempting prize is the British NHS, the third largest employer in the world (after the Chinese Red Army and the Indian State Railways).[43] The aftermath of the 2008 financial crisis has provided exactly the right conditions for such explosive growth. The need to reduce the state deficits (the debts run up by bailing out the banks) legitimates cost-cutting and the search for "efficiencies" and economies of scale. This is bolstered by a rhetoric of shrinking the state. A new model is being promoted in which the function of government is no long to deliver services but to procure them. This model has already been enthusiastically taken up by some. For instance, in October 2010 Suffolk County Council in the UK announced plans to become a "virtual council" and outsource all its services, including administrative functions, moving from a directly employed workforce of 27,000 to around 300 employees.[44] Barnet Council was already well advanced on this path, with its "Future Shape" policy, announced in 2008, which has been shown to have made few real savings, partly because of the high cost of consultancy, and leading to a drastic drop in the quality of services, as well as job losses.[45] (An even more dramatic, though smaller-scale, example is the tiny U.S. city of Maywood in Los Angeles County, which, since July 1, 2010, has had no employees whatsoever, with all its services provided by independent contractors or staff on loan from the neighboring city of Bell.)[46]

In the UK, whose coalition government provides an extreme example of this new thinking, the rhetoric surrounding these developments has been confused, on the left, by a focus on "cuts" that suggests the issue is simply one of the size of the budget devoted to public services, and, on the right, by rhetoric about the "Big Society." This rhetoric does not speak of handing public assets over directly to multinational corporations to manage (though this option is not excluded) but suggests that they will be taken over by volunteers. The *Modernising Commissioning*

Green Paper published by the UK government in 2010 quotes the Liberal Democrat manifesto commitment to "support the creation and expansion of mutuals, co-operatives, charities, and social enterprises, and enable these groups to have a much greater involvement in the running of public services." It goes on to say that "these reforms are fundamental to achieving the *Power Shift* to which this government is committed, transferring power away from central government to local communities."[47]

To what extent this is a simple smokescreen and to what extent a new role may be opening up for Non-Governmental Organizations (NGOs) in the provision of services is a moot point. Globally, the role of NGOs has changed considerably in recent years. Not only are many in partnership with multinational corporations in varying degrees of closeness (for instance, the Aga Khan Foundation provides nursing training in Tanzania funded by Johnson and Johnson),[48] but many NGOs are entirely funded by multinationals. For example the New Citizen Life Center, which provides health services and help with finding employment to destitute migrant workers in the Guijing migrant village in Pudong, on the outskirts of Shanghai in China, receives all its money from Glaxo Smith Kline, where it serves to help promote the company's products as well as to project a positive image of the company in particular, and of capitalism in general.[49] It seems likely that a similar blurring of roles will increasingly take place elsewhere. Even if services are run by independent NGOs, it is unclear to whom they will be accountable, and how. In the short term, the involvement of voluntary organizations may soften and humanize the impact of the changes; in the longer term, it seems likely that multinational companies will end up taking over the running of any operations likely to be profitable, simply by exploiting the economies of scale they can achieve. There is little question that the main impact of the new approach will be a massive transfer of public assets to corporations that can use them to generate profit. In the process, the public sector workforce will be subsumed into a larger mass of interchangeable labor: dispensable, precarious, and—since workers will increasingly be employed by bodies with intermediate positions in shifting global value chains—without a stable framework for collective representation and negotiation.

This situation is not without its contradictions. For the state, there are tensions between its role in attracting and controlling capital on its territory on the one hand and, on the other, its role in opening up a new field of expansion for capital. Within national ruling elites, there are tensions between those who want a smaller role for governments *tout court* and those (representing the companies that profit from supplying public services) who would like to see an enlarged public sphere, albeit one that is opened up for profit. There are also contradictions between the national interest in preventing unemployment from reaching unmanageable levels and the interest of global companies in searching out the cheapest workforce, wherever it may be based. What is clear, however, is that if workers are to claw back any returns for the working class from the next wave of accumulation (based as it is on the expropriation of their own past collective efforts at redistribution), new forms of organization will be required: forms of organization that recognize the common interests of a global proletariat, with globally organized employers.

7. The Underpinnings of Class in the Digital Age

Living, Labor, and Value

As Marxism has segued in and out of vogue, there is hardly a Marxian concept that has not at some time been questioned as anachronistic in the light of the transformations in economic and political conditions that have occurred over the last century and a half. The current renewal of interest in Marx's ideas is no exception. It is indeed no easy task to apply theoretical concepts developed in the mid-nineteenth century to a world where capitalism has penetrated every region and every aspect of life, where the pace of technological change is so rapid that labor processes are obsolescent within months of being introduced, and where the division of labor is so intricate that no single worker has any chance of grasping it in its full complexity. Divisions between manual and non-manual work dissolve and are reconstituted, the boundaries between production, distribution, and consumption melt away, and, though some paid work morphs into unpaid work, new jobs and new economic activities are generated from areas of life that were traditionally seen as beyond the scope of any market. In the suck and blow of commodification, the abstract becomes concrete and the concrete abstract, casting doubt on conceptual categories that formerly seemed self-evident. It may seem that we need new definitions of the most basic concepts used by Karl Marx, including "class," "commodity," and "labor."

One current idea that has attracted considerable support, especially among the young, is the notion that the idea of a working class defined by its direct relationship to production is outmoded. Since all aspects of life, such arguments go, have been drawn into the scope of the capitalist cash nexus in some way, all those who are not actually part of the capitalist class must be regarded as part of an undifferentiated "multitude." In Michael Hardt and Antonio Negri's formulation, this multitude takes the place of a working class, and according to Guy Standing, a "precariat" constitutes a new class in and for itself alongside the traditional proletariat.[1] Standing does not attempt to locate this precariat with any precision in relation to capitalist production processes. However, many of the followers of Hardt and Negri have engaged in elaborate attempts to do so in relation to the multitude. Two questions in particular have puzzled them: What sorts of commodities are being produced by members of this multitude?[2] And how does the value produced by this labor accrue to capital?

In these debates particular attention has been paid to the value created online by "virtual" or "digital" labor. In the field that is becoming known as Internet studies, there have recently been energetic debates about digital labor and how it should be conceptualized.[3] These debates have addressed the increasingly blurred boundaries between "work" and "play," encapsulated in the term "playbour,"[4] and between production and consumption—"prosumption"[5] and "co-creation"[6]—discussed the problematic category of "free labor,"[7] and questioned whether such labor, paid or unpaid, can be regarded as producing surplus value and whether it is "exploitative" or "alienated." With the exception of Andrew Ross, few of these authors have drawn parallels with other forms of labor carried out offline. Yet many of the questions they raise apply much more generally to labor under capitalism. These debates thus provide a useful starting point for investigating the labor theory of value itself, and how—or, some would wonder, even if—it can be applied in twenty-first-century conditions.

This essay argues that it is still possible to apply Marx's theory in current conditions, to define what is, or is not, a commodity, to identify the point of production of such commodities, whether material or immaterial, and to define the global working class in relation to these production processes. In order to do so, it is necessary to reexamine the labor theory of value in all its dimensions. I pay particular attention to "digital" or "virtual" labor not only because it is currently attracting so much attention, but also because online labor is particularly difficult to conceptualize. It is thus a fertile source of cases against which to test more general hypotheses. If a theory can apply here, then it should be more generally applicable. The aim of doing this is to enable a mapping of the working class across the whole economy by applying the theory more broadly (as Marx did). This is an important task, in my view, because without a clear sense of which workers are engaged directly in the antagonistic relation to capital that characterizes commodity production, and without identifying where that point of production is located, it is impossible to identify strategies that will enable labor to confront capital where it is possible to exercise some power to shape the future in its own interests.

LABOR AND CAPITALISM

The labor theory of value is the knot at the heart of Marx's conceptualization of capitalism as a social relationship. It integrally links three things: workers' need for subsistence, their labor, and the surplus value expropriated from the results of that labor, without which capital cannot be accumulated or capitalism perpetuated. The expropriation of labor is the act of violence at the heart of this relationship. It is the worker's labor time that constitutes the bone that is fought over when a worker is employed, so an understanding of how and under what circumstances this expropriation takes place is critical to an understanding both of capitalism as a system and of which workers can be said to belong to the working class. The knot cannot be undone: each rope is essential to holding the system together. Nevertheless, it seems necessary to examine it, strand by strand, so that we can grasp how it is put together, what tightens it, and what enables new threads to be drawn in or existing ones more elaborately entangled.

In its basic form, the argument is remarkably simple: the worker, obliged to do so in order to subsist, works a given number of hours for the capitalist, producing a certain value as a result. Some of this value is essential to cover the cost of subsistence, and the hours worked to produce this value, "necessary labor time," are (usually) reimbursed. The remainder, "surplus value," is appropriated by the capitalist to distribute as profit and invest in new means of production. On close examination, however, just about every element of this simple story turns out to be open to question. What, exactly, is "labor"? And, more particularly, what labor is productive of surplus value? How is "subsistence" to be defined? Does it include only what the individual worker needs to survive, or does it also include what is required for the sustenance of his or her entire household? If we cannot define subsistence precisely, how can we possibly calculate necessary labor time? And, just because all value within capitalism ultimately derives from the results of human labor applied to the earth's raw materials, does this mean that all value that accrues to individual capitalists is necessarily surplus value?

The current debates around "digital labor" skim past some of these questions and oversimplify others. This essay will not attempt to rewrite Marx's entire theory. Rather, it will take some of the questions raised in these debates about digital labor as starting points for examining the factors that will have to be taken into account in any modern elaboration of Marx's theory, an elaboration that will, in my view, be an essential precondition for understanding the new class formations that are emerging in the twenty-first century in all their complex and contradictory dimensions. I will do this by attempting to unravel the three strands—*living* (or subsistence), *labor*, and *value*—in order to categorize their separate components. I will do this in reverse order, reflecting the priorities of current debates in this field, looking first at value, then at labor, and finally at subsistence. These concepts are all well used and difficult to reemploy without bringing along a large freight of associated meanings, both intended and unintended. So it is perhaps useful to begin with two explanatory notes.

The first concerns terminology. In advanced capitalist societies, not only is the division of labor extremely complex but so, too, is the distribution of wealth. Workers' subsistence is achieved not only as a direct result of waged labor but also via redistribution through the financial system (in the form of credit, private insurance, and pension schemes, etc.) and through the state (in a monetary form through tax and Social Security systems, and in kind by means of state-provided services). In such a context, the direct connection between labor and value can be obscured. It is common for analysts to follow Marx in classifying labor as "productive" or "unproductive" (of surplus value). The approach I adopt in this essay draws on insights from feminism and makes a slightly different distinction. This is a distinction between labor that is productive for capitalism as a whole, which can be termed "reproductive," and labor that is directly productive for individual capitalists, which, for lack of a better term, I have named "directly productive." I draw a further distinction between work that is paid and work that is unpaid.

A typology of labor based on the intersection of these two variables (reproductive/productive and paid/unpaid) is summarized in the table on page 155.

Dependent though it is on other forms of labor for its reproduction, the quintessential form of labor that characterizes capitalism is labor that *both* produces value for capitalist enterprises *and* produces the income necessary for the worker's survival. This is work whose very performance contains within itself the contestation of labor time between worker and capitalist and at whose heart lies the wrench of expropriation, the experience of which Marx described as "alienation" (a term that has, unfortunately, become so contaminated with other meanings that it can no longer be used with the precision with which Marx employed it). And this is therefore the work that lies at the core of the accumulation process. The workplace is not, of course, the only place that labor confronts capital. But because capital cannot be accumulated without workers' consent, it is the site at which labor has the greatest potential power to wrest concessions from capital (without resorting to bloodshed).

The term "waged labor" encompasses work that Marx would have designated as both productive and unproductive. It also excludes various forms of labor (piecework, freelance work, etc.) paid in non-wage forms, which contribute directly both to capital accumulation and workers' subsistence. Defining labor only in terms of whether or not it is productive, in Marx's sense, ignores the reality that (as will be discussed below) there is a considerable amount of unpaid labor that produces value directly for capital without contributing to the worker's subsistence. Conversely, there is paid labor that contributes to subsistence without creating value directly for capital. After spending some time considering a range of alternatives—including "contested productive labor," "alienated productive labor," "directly productive labor," and "productive waged labor"—I have, for the purposes of this essay, decided to use a shorthand term to distinguish it from other forms of productive and waged labor. Drawing on the metaphor I used to describe the labor theory of value, I refer to it in this essay as labor which is "inside the knot." This is the labor classified in Quadrant C in the table.

Labor "inside the knot" in this definition is labor carried out directly for a capitalist employer by a worker who is dependent on this labor for subsistence and is therefore a front-line adversary in the struggle between capital and labor over how much labor time should be exchanged for how much money. This may seem like a somewhat narrow definition. It is indeed the sort of definition

	Paid labor	*Unpaid* labor
Reproductive: productive for society/ capitalism in general	A Public administration and public service work (including NGOs); individually provided private services.	B Domestic labor: childcare, household maintenance, etc., including non-market cultural activities
Directly productive: for individual capitalist enterprises	C Commodity production, including distribution	D Consumption work – substituting the unpaid labor of consumers for that of paid service and distribution workers.

Labor: A Schematic Typology

that was much criticized in the 1960s and 1970s for excluding large groups of workers who often saw themselves as part of the working class, including public sector workers and some service workers, whose relationship to production was indirect (workers who belong in Quadrant A in this diagram). In using it here, I am not arguing that such workers are not unproductive. On the contrary, many of the tasks they perform are essential for the reproduction of labor. However, these workers' exposure to the coercive logic of capitalism may be somewhat mitigated, either because they are working under older forms of employment (for instance as domestic servants, independent artisans or other petty commodity producers) or because they are employed by the state to provide as yet uncommodified services.

These forms of labor still exist, of course, but, as I argued in chapter 6, in the current wave of commodification these forms of work are diminishing and the workers who carried them out are rapidly being drawn "inside the knot."[8] In other words, the commodification of public services has produced a major shift of labor from Quadrant A to Quadrant C in the diagram.

This is not the only movement that is occurring.[9] The more general commodification of consumer goods and services has also involved large shifts from Quadrant B to Quadrant D, transforming the nature of unpaid work from the direct production of use values for household members to the purchasing of commodities in the market, involving a direct relationship with capitalist production and distribution activities.

In a further twist, there has also been a shift of labor from Quadrant C to Quadrant D as capitalist production and distribution companies have reduced their labor costs, increasing the exploitation of their paid workers by externalizing more and more tasks onto consumers who have to carry them out as unpaid self-service activities.

In a parallel process, austerity measures are also leading to a shift of activities from Quadrant A to Quadrant B, which in turn puts more pressure on the further shift from B to C.

Thus while labor "inside the knot" constitutes a subset of all labor, it is a subset that is rapidly expanding to become the overwhelming majority of paid labor.

My second cautionary note concerns the danger of extrapolation from a typology of labor to a typology of workers and hence to a class typology. Though part of my aim is to classify different forms of labor in their relation both to capital accumulation and workers' subsistence, I do not intend in so doing to produce a classification of *workers* that can be read off in any simple manner from this typology. Most workers engage in several different kinds of labor, paid and unpaid, both simultaneously and over the course of their lives, crossing these simple categories. Even more important, most workers live in households where different kinds of labor are carried out by different household members, some of whom, at any given time, may be unemployed. Whether or not members of such households perceive themselves, or can be perceived by others, as belonging to the working class is a large question. In my conclusion I will attempt to sketch out some of the ways it might be possible to map working classes in the twenty-first century drawing on this analysis. But the analysis of labor constitutes only a small first step in that larger process, and this exercise is necessarily speculative.

"DIGITAL LABOR" AND MATERIAL ECONOMIES

Before embarking on this analysis, it is worth noting that digital labor cannot be regarded as a discrete form of labor, separated hermetically from the rest of the economy. As I have argued in the past, the existence of a separately visible sphere of non-manual labor is not evidence of a new "knowledge-based," "immaterial," or "weightless" realm of economic activity.[10] It is simply an expression of the growing complexity of the division of labor, with a fragmentation of activities into separate tasks, both "mental" and "manual," increasingly capable of being dispersed geographically and contractually to different workers who may be barely aware of one another's existence. This is a continuing process, with each task subject to further divisions between more creative and/or controlling functions on the one hand, and more routine, repetitive ones on the other.

Furthermore, though there has clearly been an enormous expansion in non-manual work, both routine and de-skilled and otherwise, it remains a minority of all labor. The growing visibility of apparently dematerialized labor, dependent on information and communications technologies, has sometimes served to obscure the reality that this "virtual" activity is dependent on a highly material basis of physical infrastructure and manufactured commodities, most of which are produced out of the sight of observers in developed economies, in the mines of Africa and Latin America, the sweatshops of China, and other places in the developing world. Without the generation of power, cables, satellites, computers, switches, mobile phones, and thousands of other material products, the extraction of the raw materials that make up these commodities, the launching of satellites into space to carry their signals, the construction of the buildings in which they are designed and assembled and from which they are marketed, and the manufacture and operation of the vehicles in which they are distributed, the Internet could not be accessed by anyone.

Although 20 percent of the world's 100 largest transnational corporations are now service companies, it should not be forgotten that 80 percent are not.[11] And, according to UNCTAD, in 2012 it was manufacturing companies that were expanding their foreign investment the fastest.[12] The physical production of material commodities is still capitalism's preferred method for generating profit; it is still growing, and it seems likely to continue to employ the largest proportion of the world's workforce.

There is, moreover, a continuum between tasks that mainly involve the exercise of physical strength or dexterity and those that involve mental agility, engagement, or concentration. Few jobs do not require workers to bring their own knowledge, judgment, and intelligence to the task at hand, and even fewer do not involve some physical activity, even if this just entails speaking, listening, watching a screen, or tapping keys.

That said, a large and growing proportion of the workforce *is* involved in performing "digital labor" whose products are intangible, much of it low-paid and menial. And many members of this workforce are descended from or cohabiting with workers who would by any definition be assigned to the working class. It is therefore important to understand what role their labor plays in global capitalism, what the composition of this workforce is, how it is changing, and what class allegiances these workers might express.

VALUE

Put simply, it could be said that there are three main ways that enterprises generate profit under capitalism, the first two of which also existed under other systems. These are rent, trade, and the generation of surplus value through commodity production. Because it is the paradigmatic form of value generation under capitalism, it is commodity production that receives the most attention from Marxian analysts. If value is observably being generated from some activity, the tendency is to search for the commodity at its source. If a commodity cannot easily be identified, or if it does not appear to be produced by extracting surplus value from paid workers, then it is sometimes concluded that this means Marx's labor theory of value does not apply and is either outmoded or in need of adaptation. However, before leaping to the conclusion that entirely new theories are needed to explain new activities that do not seem to fit the earlier models, such as online activities, it is worth analyzing them in relation to traditional forms of value generation to see whether they fit these categories.

RENT

The ways in which commercially mediated online activities seem to encroach indiscriminately on work, leisure, consumption, and personal relationships draws attention to the extent to which capitalist relations have spread into all aspects of life, or as Marx put it, "In the modern world, personal relations flow purely out of relations of production and exchange," encouraging broad-ranging speculation about how the monetization of online exchanges can be understood and theorized.[13] The starting point for many of the current discussions about the value generated on the Internet is the indisputable reality that online companies like Google and Facebook are hugely profitable. If they are making profits, it is then argued, this must be because some commodity is being produced, which in turn begs the question what precisely these commodities might be and whose labor is producing them. In the case of Google and Facebook, the main source of income is revenues from advertising, which can be targeted with great precision as a result of the ever-more sophisticated analysis of data generated by users. Here, Dallas Smythe's concept of the "audience commodity"[14] has been seized on by a number of commentators, including Christian Fuchs.[15] Originally developed as part of a Marxian attempt to understand the economics of advertising in commercial radio and television, this concept portrays the media audience as the commodity that is sold to advertisers to generate revenue: "Because audience power is produced, sold, purchased and consumed, it commands a price and is a commodity."[16] Fuchs applies this logic to the Internet: "The productive labor time that is exploited by capital . . . involves . . . all of the time that is spent online by the users." He goes on to say that "the rate of exploitation converges towards infinity if workers are unpaid. They are infinitely exploited." Other contributors to the digital labor debate suggest that "reputation"[17] or even life itself, produced by "bio-labor,"[18] have become commodities.

While Smythe's concept has undoubtedly opened up useful insights into the nature of the mass media, it has also led to much confusion. The underlying assumption among Smythe's followers seems to be that the term "commodity" can be used to refer to anything that can be bought and sold. There is a certain circular logic operating here. Since Marx declares that "commodities are nothing but crystallized labor" and that "a good only has a value because labor is objectified or materialized in it," then it must follow, according to this logic, that anything described as a commodity must be the result of productive labor.[19] But how useful is such a broad conception of the term?

It seems to me that in order to understand the distinctive nature of the commodity form under capitalism a somewhat different definition needs to be used. I have defined commodities elsewhere as "standardized products or services for sale in a market whose sale will generate profits that increase in proportion to the scale of production" (all else being equal).[20] This definition singles out capitalist commodities as fundamentally different from those produced under other systems. A traditional carpenter making chairs and selling them directly to the public makes more or less the same profit on each chair. The capitalist who opens a factory and employs workers to mass-produce chairs has to make an investment in machinery, buildings, and so on and will not make a profit on the first chair, but the more chairs that are produced in that factory, the greater the profit on any given one. This gives the chairs produced in the factory a fundamentally different character from those produced individually by a single artisan in relation to their value. There are a number of services, including intangible ones (such as insurance policies or software programs), that have the same character as commodities. It is the social relations under which they are produced—the coerced labor of waged workers, under the control of the capitalist—that gives them this character.[21] Such a definition of commodity inverts the logic of Smythe's followers. It takes as its starting point the nature of the capitalist-labor relationship rather than the fact that something is being sold.

If they do not derive from the sale of commodities, how can we understand the profits made by online social networking or search engine companies? An alternative explanation, and one that has long antecedents in the offline world, is that they derive from rent. A simple historical example of a similar way of generating income could be provided by a street market where the rent charged for a stall-space is higher in areas where the most customers (or the richest customers) will pass by. Bricks-and-mortar examples can be found on New York's Fifth Avenue, London's Oxford Street, or any other street with a large and lucrative footfall: the more well-trafficked the site, the higher the rent. For well over a century, properties that border busy highways have been able to make money by renting space for billboards. Don't online companies simply follow the same model albeit with sites that are virtual rather than paved, and rather more sophisticated means of identifying the most lucrative customers and gaining intelligence about their desires? The value that accrues to the social networking and search engine sites does indeed ultimately derive from surplus value produced by labor. But this is the labor of the workers who produced the commodities that are advertised on these sites, not the labor of the people who use the sites.[22]

Some participants in the digital labor debate, such as Adam Arvidsson and Eleanor Colleoni, dispute Fuchs's notion that social media users are producing surplus value.[23] They, too, argue that the value generated can be more properly regarded as rent. However, they use the term "rent" to refer to the value that accrues to financial investors in these companies. But in this respect they do not say what it is that makes online companies different from any other companies that are quoted on stock exchanges and attract financial investments. In attempting to classify what, precisely, it is that generates the value that attracts such investors, they develop an explanation whereby "social media platforms like Facebook function as channels by means of which affective investments on the part of the multitude can be translated into objectified forms of abstract affect that support financial valuations." They further argue that such companies gain their share of "socially produced surplus value" through "the ability to attract affective investments . . . from the multitude or the global public."[24] This somewhat convoluted model sidesteps the rather more prosaic question of who is paying whom for what in order to generate the return on investment for the shareholders. It can, in my opinion, be rather simply answered by saying that it is the advertisers (producers of commodities for sale) who are paying the social media or search engine companies for the opportunity to advertise to their users. This is not to deny that social media sites do not incidentally also facilitate other forms of labor that could be regarded as more directly productive. These will be discussed below.

There are, of course, a number of ways that value is generated online other than through the use of search engine or social media sites. Many other online activities rely on rent for the generation of income. These include a variety of other sites that rely on advertising revenue, but also sites that charge rents to their users for access to information (such as online databases), sites from which copyright music or videos can be purchased and downloaded (such as iTunes), companies that sell software licenses online, and online games for which subscriptions have to be bought (on the same principle as software licenses).

Other sites can be regarded as essentially online equivalents of offline businesses that generate income from rent. These include online marketplaces (such as eBay), dating sites (such as eHarmony or Match.com), online employment agencies that match freelance workers to employers (such as oDesk or Elance), price comparison sites, online travel booking or accommodation finding sites (such as Expedia), or various forms of peer-to-peer services allowing people to find bed-and-breakfast accommodation (such as Airbnb) or car shares (such as Lyft). The connection with offline businesses is often evident here. For example, one of the largest of the online peer-to-peer car rental services, RelayRides, was launched with funding from GM Ventures (the investment arm of General Motors) in 2011 and has now been acquired by Zipcar, which in turn was acquired by Avis in January 2013.[25]

Whatever the specific mix of sources of revenue, most of the profit of such enterprises comes from some combination of charging usage or commission fees to service providers and/or service users and/or advertisers—in other words, rent. It is interesting to note that some of these sites seem to be enabling the development of new forms of petty commodity production and rentier activity or allowing older forms to survive offline. Etsy, for example, makes it possible for individuals to sell craft products in the online equivalent of a crafts market. Airbnb lets them make an income from renting out rooms in their homes for bed and breakfast (taking a percentage of the cost). Peer-to-peer car rental services enable people to provide taxi services or charge others to borrow their cars.

TRADE

Trade involves acquiring something at one price (including stealing it) and selling it a higher price, making a profit in the process. Some forms of stealing, such as the appropriation of other people's intellectual property, may take place online. These include the reselling of captured images or music or the plagiarism of text for sale or some more elaborate forms of theft that are currently emerging, such as the exploitation of the unpaid labor of language learners to obtain free translation of Web content by the website Duolingo.com, or reCAPTCHA's use of users' attempts to decode distorted images of letters and numbers—that cannot be recognized by automatic optical scanning systems.[26]

However, there are also a very large number of companies that sell online (Amazon being probably the most famous) in a manner that replicates offline commercial trade. Indeed many established merchants now buy and sell both online and offline. Although there may be some blurring of traditional boundaries among the distribution activities of manufacturers, wholesalers, and retailers, and some labor processes may be rather different, there is nothing mysterious about how value is generated here. The scale of many of these companies, and the fact that they have had to put extensive infrastructure in place for processing payments internationally, has meant that some of them have been able to diversify into rental activities that have in turn created the basis for new forms of commodity production, discussed in the next section.

COMMODITY PRODUCTION

This brings us to the final category: value generated from the production of commodities. Here, the analyst seeking to isolate the role of digital labor in value creation is faced with considerable challenges. The spread of computing across most sectors of the economy, combined with the near-universal use of telecommunications, means that few economic activities do *not* involve some element of digital labor, whether they take place in farms, factories, warehouses, offices, shops, homes, or in moving vehicles. Furthermore, these activities are linked with one another in complex chains that cross the boundaries of firms, sectors, regions, and countries. Tracing the connection of any given activity back to its origins, or forward to the final commodity to whose production it has contributed, is no easy task. Nevertheless, it is by no means impossible. One useful approach here is to analyze economic activities in functional terms.[27]

The functions of research and development and design, for instance, clearly make direct inputs to the development of new commodities (or the adaptation of older ones). Much of the labor involved in these activities nowadays comes into the category of digital labor in that it involves computer-based tools and/or is delivered in digital form to the workers who will take it forward to the production stage. The same goes for activities whose purpose is to develop content for books, films, CDs, or other cultural products. Here some activities may be more directly "digital" than others: actors or musicians, for instance, may be performing in a manner that is "live," but if the end result is going to be incorporated into a reproducible commodity then their functional relation to capital is the same as that of fellow workers sitting at screens or mixing desks.[28] Digital labor is also implicated in a variety of ways in production processes, whether this entails the operation of digitally controlled tools, the maintenance of software, the generation of immaterial products or the supervision of other workers engaged in these processes.

When it comes to "service" activities it is useful—though increasingly difficult—to make a general distinction among those that contribute directly to production (such as cleaning the factory floor or servicing the machines); those that contribute to the maintenance or management of the workforce (such as processing payroll data or staff recruitment or training); those that contribute to the more general management of the enterprise (including financial management); those that are involved in activities connected with purchasing, sales, and marketing; and those that are involved in distribution. All of these categories include activities that are carried out online and/or using a combination of information and communications technologies. They are, however, becoming more and more difficult to tell apart, for several interconnected reasons.

The first of these is the increasingly generic nature of many labor processes. Workers inputting numerical data on a keyboard, for instance, may be doing it for a bank, a government department, or a manufacturing company, for purposes entirely unknown to them. Call center operators may be using standard scripts to deal with sales, customer services, debt collection, government inquiries, fundraising, or a variety of other functions, cutting across any neat classification system that would allow them to be sorted into different categories by function. Software engineers may be working on the development of new products, or the maintenance of existing ones.

Closely linked with this form of standardization is the growing propensity of such activities to be outsourced, often to companies that bundle together a number of different functions for different clients into clusters of activities carried out in shared service centers. The possibility for these and other services to be carried out online has further blurred the distinction between services provided to businesses and those provided directly to final customers. If everyone can order goods online, to be delivered to the door from a central warehouse, then the distinction between "wholesale" and "retail" becomes an artificial one. Similarly, a growing range of standardized immaterial products, ranging from software licenses to bank accounts to insurance policies, can be sold as readily to individuals as to companies.

The existence of online platforms through which labor can be coordinated has led to the development of an extreme form of subdivision of tasks, sometimes known as "micro-labor," "crowd work,"[29] or "crowd-sourcing."[30] These new forms of labor include "pay-per-click" work whereby workers are paid by commercial companies to "Like" their Facebook posts or blog entries, or platforms like Amazon's Mechanical Turk, whose users are paid a few cents to perform a variety of very small tasks, so fragmented that workers are very unlikely to understand what relation any given task has to the final commodity to which it contributes.

If such activities, however dispersed, are carried out by paid workers, in the employ of enterprises set up to make a profit, then they can unproblematically be assigned to the category of work that directly produces surplus value for capital—labor "inside the knot." However, as the borderlines between production, distribution, and consumption become increasingly fuzzy and the same activity can be carried out interchangeably by paid and unpaid workers, this simple position needs some modification. Marx was somewhat ambivalent about distribution labor, regarding transport workers as productive, but not retail workers. However, at one point in the *Grundrisse* he asserted that the whole process of bringing a product to market should be regarded as productive labor: "Economically considered, the spatial condition, the bringing of the product to the market, belongs to the production process itself. The product is really finished only when it is on the market."[31] Some would disagree, but I believe that if Marx were alive today and saw the complexity of the distribution processes of modern capitalist enterprises he would assert this point more strongly.

Following this logic, a wide range of functions to be found in a modern corporation can be assigned to this directly productive category, including marketing, logistics management, distribution, transport, customer service, retail and wholesale sales (whether online or offline), and delivery—in short, the whole supply chain from factory gate (or software development site) to the final consumer should be regarded as productive labor. But what happens when the customer's unpaid labor is substituted for that of the productive waged worker? What if, for instance, you go and fetch a purchase in person from the store or warehouse? Or design your own product, selecting a unique combination of standard features from a website? And what, exactly, is the difference between booking your own holiday via a website, keying in your own data, and doing so over the phone to a (paid) call-center operator who keys it in on your behalf? In the latter case, the labor falls comfortably into what is traditionally regarded as the "productive" category. But what about the former? In my view, all these activities should be regarded as productive. However, only those carried out by paid workers fall "inside the knot" whereby their relationship to capital is both direct and, actually or potentially, contested.

LABOR

Any attempt to categorize different forms of labor has to begin by confronting the extraordinarily difficult question of what labor actually is. The word itself covers a vast spectrum of meanings from the physical exertion of giving birth at one extreme to formal participation in employment, or the political representation of people who do so, at the other. If we take it to refer to activities that are actually or potentially reimbursed by wages in a "labor market," then we have to include a large range of activities that most people carry out without pay, including sex, caring for children, cooking, cleaning, gardening, singing, making people laugh, and holding forth on topics that interest us.

If we apply a more subjective filter and try to exclude activities that are carried out for pleasure, then we are confronted with the awkward reality that the same activity may be experienced as a chore or a joy under differing circumstances and, furthermore, that some activities, paid or unpaid, may be both onerous and enjoyable simultaneously. The baby, for instance, may give you a beaming smile while its smelly diaper is being changed; a truck driver's long lonely journey may suddenly bestow a heart-stoppingly beautiful glimpse of landscape; hard physical work in harsh surroundings may engender a camaraderie among workers that leaves a warm glow long after the muscle ache has subsided; solving a tricky problem may release a sudden gush of satisfaction, even if the problem is not one's own.

Another dimension that might help to distinguish between "labor" and "pleasure" is whether the activity is carried out voluntarily or by coercion, under the direction of another person or organization. Here again what seems a simple distinction becomes remarkably difficult to apply in practice. One difficulty results from the historically determined ways in which such things as gender roles, concepts of duty, or even caste-based divisions of labor are internalized, rendering patterns of power and coercion invisible to all parties and, indeed, giving many acts of service the subjective quality of freely offered gifts of love even when objective analysis might suggest that they involve the exploitation of one person's labor by another. Coercion may also be exercised in more indirect ways. An addicted gambler, for instance, may perceive his or her compulsion as internally generated, not recognizing the societal pressures that impel it. The same could, perhaps, be said of many of the online activities that people spend so much time on, including online gaming and interacting with others on social media sites. It is perhaps some inkling of these social pressures that leads so many commentators in the digital media debates to insist that these unpaid activities are a form of "free" labor.[32]

Unpaid labor is not, of course, a new phenomenon. It has, however, received only rather fitful attention from Marxian scholars except as a kind of vestigial repository of precapitalist social relations from which waged labor later emerged. Apart from debates about slavery among historians, most of the attention paid to unpaid labor until recently was in the context of what could loosely be called "reproductive labor," in particular in feminist debates during the 1970s. In these discussions, the main question raised was whether unpaid domestic labor or "housework" could be regarded as producing surplus value—because without it capitalism could not exist. The reproduction of the workforce depended crucially, it was argued, on unpaid labor in the home, not only for bringing up the next generation of workers but also to provide the nutrition, cleaning, and bodily maintenance services that allow the current workforce to perform effectively in the labor market. In 1976, Batya Weinbaum and Amy Bridges published a groundbreaking article in which they argued that, under monopoly capital conditions, much of this labor not only involved producing services in the home but also consuming commodities produced in the market.[33] The concept of "consumption work," in which unpaid labor is substituted for what was formerly the paid labor of distribution workers, is one that I developed further in the late 1970s and, I argue here, is relevant for understanding some of the new forms of unpaid labor that take place both on and offline.[34]

Drawing on some of this work, I propose here a somewhat rough-and-ready typology of unpaid labor in the hope that it can provide a starting point for a categorization that will bring some clarity to these debates.

The first category is the labor that is carried out independently of the market to produce use values in the home, the category of labor located in Quadrant B in the table on page 155. It is "unproductive" in the sense that it produces no direct value for capital in the form of surplus value from somebody's direct labor, but is "reproductive" in the sense that it is necessary for the reproduction of the workforce. It includes many of the tasks traditionally carried out in subsistence agriculture and housework. If someone is employed to do this kind of work by the direct user of the service (for example, a domestic servant, nanny, cleaner or gardener) that worker is, in Marx's opinion, an unproductive worker, although if they are employed via a capitalist intermediary (for example, a commercial childcare, cleaning or gardening company) then they move into the category of productive worker (in terms of the table, from Quadrant A to Quadrant C).[35] However, we are concerned here with unpaid labor. To the extent that maintaining the emotional health of a family and sustaining the social networks in which it is embedded is a necessary part of ensuring the survival of a household, then a range of non-physical activities can be included in this category, including such seemingly trivial tasks as remembering birthdays, writing letters of condolence, or arranging social get-togethers that help to produce and reproduce the solidaristic bonds that may be necessary for survival in times of crisis. It also includes acquiring the skills and habits that enable someone to be employable. Even courtship can be regarded as a necessary prelude to this family maintenance project. Many of these activities are carried out online these days; thus at least a part of online social networking activity could be assigned to this category (represented by Quadrant B). Whether or not the person carrying out this labor is exposed to advertising in the process of carrying it out is as incidental to the productivity of the labor as whether or not they might pass a billboard on the way to visit a sick grandmother or be exposed to film commercials while on a date.

The second category of unpaid labor is what I have referred to above as "consumption work" (Quadrant D). This involves the consumer taking on tasks in the market that were previously carried out by paid workers as part of the distribution processes of commodity production. Since these tasks are necessary to the distribution of these commodities, and increase the profits of the commodity-producing companies by eliminating forms of labor that were formerly paid for, there are strong arguments for categorizing this kind of work as "productive," even when it is unpaid. However, because it does not generate income directly for the worker it has to be treated differently from paid labor in relation to its contribution to subsistence, a topic to which I will return below. It is, in other words, "outside the knot." As already noted, increasing amounts of consumption work are now carried out online, with the Internet having opened up a range of new ways of externalizing labor over distance.[36]

The third category involves creative work. Here Marx made his position clear:

> Milton, for example . . . was an unproductive worker. In contrast to this, the writer who delivers hackwork for his publisher is a productive worker. Milton produced *Paradise Lost* in the way that a silkworm produces silk, as the expression of *his own* nature. Later on he sold the product for £5 and to that extent became a dealer in a commodity. . . . A singer who sings like a bird is an unproductive worker. If she sells her singing for money, she is to that extent a wage labourer or a commodity dealer. But the same singer, when engaged by an entrepreneur who has her sing in order to make money, is a productive worker, for she directly *produces* capital.[37]

According to this conception, to the extent that it is carried out for the purposes of self-expression, unpaid artistic work, such as blogging or posting one's photographs, music, or videos on the Internet, comes straightforwardly into Marx's category of "unproductive" labor (which I would prefer to regard as unpaid reproductive labor, producing social use values). If the product of this labor is subsequently sold, or stolen, to become the basis of a commodity, then this does not change that status. It is only if the worker is hired to do the work by a capitalist for a wage that it becomes productive labor in Marx's sense of the term (i.e., it moves from Quadrant B to Quadrant C). As Andrew Ross has pointed out, many artistic workers may oscillate between these forms: "Creatives have been facing this kind of choice since the eighteenth century when the onset of commercial culture markets offered them the choice of eking out a living with the scribblers on Pope's Grub Street or of building a name-recognition relationship with the fickle public."[38] The fact that the same person does both kinds of work does not, however, invalidate the distinction between them. Creative work thus has to be seen as straddling a number of different positions in the labor market, including self-employment, paid employment, and petty commodity production, leading, very often, to contradictory identities for creative workers.[39]

The same logic applies even in the much-discussed case of the "free labor" that built the Internet, much of which was designed by idealistic software developers who donated their labor for nothing in the belief that they were creating a common benefit for humankind—in other words they were producing social use value without pay, placing them in Quadrant B. As Marx said, "Labor with the same content can be both productive and unproductive."[40] In this case, it seems that although the results of their labor were appropriated by capital to incorporate into new commodities, their original unpaid labor cannot be regarded as productive in the sense of producing surplus value for capital under coercive conditions; that is, it is not "inside the knot." Rather, the value that was produced from it should more properly be put into the category of trade, which, as I noted above, also includes theft.

A fourth—but overlapping—form of unpaid labor, which is increasingly discussed, is the widespread use of unpaid internship or "voluntary" labor.[41] This, too, seems to have precedents in various forms of apprenticeship labor, such as the production of "showpieces" to impress potential employers. Situated ambiguously between education and self-promotion, it is undoubtedly used in highly exploitative ways by employers as a direct substitute for paid work. Sometimes, direct coercion is involved to oblige the worker to undertake unpaid "work placements," for instance by state job search agencies, which threaten the withdrawal of unemployment benefits from those who refuse to take them. Nevertheless, like the unpaid consumption labor already discussed, while clearly contributing value to commodity production, this form of labor plays no part in generating present income for the worker and must therefore be regarded as "outside the knot," even if it is producing value indirectly for the unpaid worker in the form of "employability." It is clear that in order to make sense of the relationship of unpaid labor to capital we have to take into account the third rope in the knot that constitutes the labor theory of value: the worker's subsistence, or "living."

LIVING

The question of how the worker pays for the cost of subsistence is surprisingly absent from most of the debates about "free" digital labor. Perhaps because the majority of the authors who have contributed to these discussions often have secure academic jobs they fail to ask how those dedicated workers who built the Internet with their free labor actually made a living. Nor, among those who advocate a "Creative Commons" on the Internet, to which all authors are supposed to donate their work for free, is it ever made clear how these authors are supposed to pay their rent and provide for their families.

Yet the labor theory of value cannot be operationalized without this information. In order to know how much surplus value is generated, and how, from any given unit of labor, we need to know the cost of that worker's reproduction, and how much of his or her working time is the "necessary labor time" required to sustain life. Only then can we see how much of the remainder is left over to be appropriated as surplus value and begin to formulate demands for its redistribution. This is not, of course, a mechanical calculation. It is perfectly possible for workers to be employed below the cost of subsistence. What does the employer care if they die, if there are plenty more where they came from? Equally, it is possible for well-organized groups of workers with scarce skills to punch above their weight and claim back from capital a higher wage than that required for bare survival—even one that allows them to employ other workers as servants. Nevertheless, capitalism as a system, in Marx's model, requires a working class that is compelled to sell its labor to survive, just as it requires capitalists who are able to employ that labor to produce commodities whose collective value on the market exceeds the total wages of the workforce required to produce them. And it is the direct experience of being obliged to contest ownership of their labor time with the employer that produces the alienation likely to lead to class consciousness. The question of "necessary labor time" therefore cannot be ducked.

But even in Marx, this is a problematic concept. One reason for this is that although workers normally enter the labor market as separate individuals, their subsistence takes place in households where several people may cohabit.[42] Because these households vary considerably in size and composition and in the number of members who engage in paid work, the same wage may have to stretch to cover the subsistence of varying numbers of people. Marx and Engels discuss the "natural" (*sic*) division of labor in the family, which they regard as a form of "latent slavery" that can even be regarded as the origin of all property.[43] From this premise, that women and children are the property of the male head of household, it is possible for them to conclude that, when women and children enter the workforce, "formerly, the sale and purchase of labor-power was a relation between free persons; now, minors or children are bought; the worker now sells wife and child—he becomes a slave-dealer."[44]

In the twenty-first century, when women make up nearly half the workforce in most developed countries and only a minority are economically inactive, such an explanation will not suffice. Every worker who enters employment needs to be separately accounted for as an individual with his or her own cost of subsistence to be raised. The fact that people cohabit with other workers can, however, mean that this "necessary labor time" should be regarded as producing a fraction, rather than the whole, of any individual's cost of subsistence. Or, in other words, that the concept of a "family wage" is redundant in most circumstances. A number of other factors have also intervened to make it difficult to identify a simple correspondence between what a person earns and what it costs for this person to survive, at least in situations where he or she is cohabiting with, or responsible for, economic dependents. These complicating factors include societal transfers in the form of pensions, welfare benefits, or tax credits, intergenerational transfers within families, remittances from migrants working abroad, and other forms of subsidy for some (or drains on the resources of others). Tax credits, the favored neoliberal model of social transfer, have played a particularly pernicious role in disguising not only the extent to which many jobs pay wages that are well below subsistence level but also in concealing from public awareness the reality that a large and growing proportion of social benefit payments go not to unemployed "scroungers" but to workers in employment.[45] Such transfers could thus be seen as having played an important role in blunting class consciousness and diverting workers' energy away from direct conflict with their employers.

Despite very real difficulties of precise calculation, it is nevertheless possible to analyze the income of any given individual in any given household and produce some estimate of how this is generated. In the case of "free labor" on the Internet, it is likely that a number of different income sources may be involved. Some of this labor may be contributed by people who are economically dependent on their parents, some by people drawing pensions or receiving some other form of welfare benefit, some by people with regular salaries from jobs that leave them with enough leisure time to blog, surf the Net, or write Wikipedia entries; some might be carried out by people (such as freelance journalists, consultants, or academics) whose jobs require them to engage in self-promotion. And others might be being supported from rents, gambling, proceeds from trade, crime, or other activities. What is clear is that they could not engage in this unpaid activity without some kind of subsidy from somewhere. Otherwise, how would they eat? Arguments that postulate the production of surplus value at a societal level from their labor seem untenable. Such arguments could also be seen as playing a similar role to societal financial transfers in diverting workers' attention away from confronting the employers directly expropriating their labor toward expressing their anger and sense of exploitation toward abstract targets, such as globalization. In failing to organize at the point of production, workers give away their strongest weapon: the power to withdraw their labor.

CLASS CONFIGURATION IN THE TWENTY-FIRST CENTURY

We live in a society where capital is highly concentrated, with most commodity production carried out by companies whose fates are largely shaped by financial investors. The commodities they produce, whether material or immaterial, are made available to us in a global marketplace, delivered through complex value chains in whose operation our own unpaid labor as consumers is increasingly implicated. Information and communications technologies have so affected the spatial and temporal division of labor that for many of us the boundaries between work and private life are inextricably muddled and few relationships are unmediated by them.

In such a situation, are not the kinds of distinctions made in this essay not ridiculously nitpicking? Should we not just accept that all of us are, in some way or another, part of a huge undifferentiated workforce, producing undifferentiated value for an undifferentiated capital?

I argue that we should not. Capitalism is a social relationship in which workers play specific roles in relation to the production of specific commodities. This relationship relies crucially on workers' consent. If we cannot understand this relationship in its specificity, we cannot identify the critical points in the processes of production and distribution at which workers' agency can be implemented to some effect. And if we cannot identify these, workers cannot understand their powers to consent to, or refuse, the specific deal on offer to them. This prevents them from actively renegotiating the terms of the deal—their only option for improving their situation. Nor can we see, without this knowledge, which groups of workers have interests in common, how these common interests might become mutually visible, or how their labor may be interconnected.

Each of the different forms of unpaid labor described above has an impact on paid labor, opening up the potential for tensions and fissures within the working class. Interns, working for nothing to make themselves employable, erode the bargaining position of paid workers in the same roles. Carrying out unpaid consumption work affects service workers by reducing overall employment levels and intensifying work through the introduction of new forms of standardization and Taylorization, leading to deteriorating working conditions. Writing Wikipedia entries, blogging, or posting video clips or photographs online without payment threatens the livelihood of journalists, researchers, or other creative workers who lack a subsidy from an academic salary or other source and rely on their creative work to provide an income. In many cases, the same people occupy several of these paid and unpaid roles in different capacities. Even more commonly, different members of the same household may be doing so. To regard unpaid workers as scabs who are undermining paid workers is of course much too simplistic, ignoring the imperatives that propel these behaviors and the broader reality that exploitation takes place in all of them, albeit in different forms. But an analysis that equates a common exploitation with an identical role in the generation of surplus value, and collapses all these separate positions into a common collective identity as a "multitude" makes it impossible to identify the point of production: the point where workers have the power to challenge capital—the center of the knot.

Starting from a detailed analysis of how value chains are structured, it is possible to begin to sketch out the lineaments of the class configuration that might confront us in coming years. However, this exercise has to be embarked on with extreme caution because, as noted earlier, many of us are engaged simultaneously or consecutively in a number of different forms of labor, with different relations to capital, or live in households where multiple forms of labor take place.

Leaving aside the rural populations that still subsist, at least in part, from their own direct labor on the land, the largest group in this emerging labor landscape, and by far the most rapidly-growing, is that of workers "inside the knot": those who are employed by capitalist enterprises producing commodities, both material and immaterial. Many of these workers have been sucked into directly capitalist labor relations comparatively recently, coming to this work as migrants from the countryside or from other countries, being transferred from public sector employment, or recruited from a previous existence in petty commodity production. Not all of them have the status of permanent employees, with many paid by piecework rates or employed on a casual or temporary basis. They are, nevertheless, productive workers, directly producing surplus value. However, the ways in which their labor processes connect with each other are not obvious.

A product like a smartphone contains within it the results of the labor of miners, assembly-line workers, chemical workers, designers, engineers, call-center workers, invoice clerks, cleaners, and many more. Scattered in different countries, with different occupational and social identities, these workers may not perceive themselves as having anything whatsoever in common. Indeed, they may believe their interests to be directly opposed to each other. If and when they organize themselves, this might be on the basis of skill, occupation, or the company they work for, but it might also be on the basis of a shared regional, linguistic, or cultural identity, a shared political history or a response to a shared form of discrimination. What forms of solidarity or shared consciousness might emerge from these forms of organization is an open question.

Another open question is the extent to which managerial, professional, and technical workers within these value chains will identify with other workers rather than aligning themselves with the employer. These are volatile occupational groups, made up of people who, in the accelerating speed of technological change and economic restructuring, find many of their labor processes undergoing standardization and de-skilling even while new opportunities to become managers are emerging. On the one hand, their employers want to nurture them as sources of innovation; on the other, they want to cheapen their labor and drive up their productivity. Caught between these two contradictory imperatives, they may be put into a position where they have to decide whether to continue to internalize management priorities and take the pain, to leave, to look for individualistic solutions, or to throw in their lot with other workers and resist.

Alongside, and overlapping with, this explosively growing body of workers "inside the knot" of capitalism are other groups less directly involved in capitalist social relations. These include people patching together a living out of petty commodity production, small-scale rent, or trade, a class that Marx assumed would die out but appears to have been given a new lease of life by the Internet, although it is doubtful whether such sources of income can ever supply a sustainable livelihood for more than a minority of the population. In many cases, it seems likely that this way of earning a living, often cobbled together from several different kinds of economic activity, is a transitional one, adopted by people who have been displaced from the formal labor market, or have not yet managed to enter it. It is not new. Working-class biographies have always thrown up many examples of people making ends meet by taking in lodgers, child-minding, pet-breeding, or making small items for sale. But it cannot be taken for granted that all such people will necessarily identify their interests with those of workers "inside the knot."

Groups that are "outside the knot" also include people involved in paid reproduction work: public sector workers in the increasingly rare fields of service provision that remain uncommodified; domestic servants; and other service workers who are not directly involved in the market (such as workers in the voluntary sector). Their work is, of course, necessary for the reproduction of capitalism, but it is "outside the knot" according to my earlier definition. Again, these groups cover a diverse range of social identities and may not perceive themselves as having interests in common, either with each other or with workers "inside the knot."

Added to these are large numbers of people who are not paid workers but who nevertheless also produce value, either in the form of reproduction, such as unpaid childcare or housework, or (externalized) production, in the form of consumption work. Many of these will be women, and their unpaid status may place them into relations of dependency on paid workers or on the state. History has given us many examples of reproduction workers throwing in their lot with the production workers their lives are linked with, for instance in the organization of miners' wives in the UK coal-miners' strike in the 1980s, and of consumption workers acting in solidarity with production workers, for instance in the consumer-based Clean Clothes Campaign that organizes petitions and boycotts to improve working conditions for garment workers.[46]

These are broad categories and a much more detailed mapping of the composition of these groups and their interrelationships with one another will be necessary to predict the class configuration that will confront us globally in the twenty-first century. Tedious though it may be to unravel the complexities of global value chains and position our labor processes in relation to them, this seems to be an absolutely necessary task if we are to learn how this system might be changed, act collectively to change it, and start to imagine what alternatives might be possible.

Notes

Introduction

Some parts of this chapter are drawn from my introduction to "Working Online, Living Offline: Labor in the Internet Age," *Work Organisation, Labour and Globalisation* 7/1, 2013, 1–11.

1. B. Lanoo, *Overview of ICT Energy Consumption,* Report to the European Commission from the Network of Excellence in Internet Science, 2013, http://www.tech-pundit.com/.
2. M. P. Mill, *The Cloud Begins with Coal,* Report to the National Mining Association and American Coalition for Clean Coal Energy report, Digital Power Group, 2013.
3. For example, B. Jessop, *State Theory: Putting the Capitalist State in Its Place* (Cambridge: Polity, 1990).
4. For example, S. A. Marglin and J. B. Schor, *The Golden Age of Capitalism: Reinterpreting the Postwar Experience* (Oxford: Oxford University Press, 1992).
5. For example, A. Lipietz and D. Macey, *Mirages and Miracles: Crisis in Global Fordism* (London: Verso, 1987).
6. J. Fourastie, *Les Trente Glorieuses, ou la révolution invisible de 1946 à 1975* (Paris: Fayard. 1979).
7. In the EU, for instance, the first *Utilities Directive* (90/351) removed market access barriers to energy, telecommunications, transport and water, and in 1992 the *Services Directive* established the principle that public services should be procured openly on the market.
8. D. Raggett, J. Lam, and I. Alexander, *HTML 3: Electronic Publishing on the World Wide Web* (Boston: Addison-Wesley, 1996).

9. UNCTAD, *World Investment Report 2004: The Shift toward Services* (New York and Geneva: UNCTAD, 2004).
10. CNN, "Global 500," *CNN Money,* July 30, 2013, http://money.cnn.com/magazines/fortune/global500/2011/countries/China.html.
11. *Financial Times, FT 500,* 2013,http://www.ft.com/indepth/ft500.
12. "World's 500 Largest Corporations: In 2013 the Chinese Are Rising," Forbes, July 17, 2013, http://www.forbes.com/sites/panosmourdoukoutas/2013/07/17/worlds-500-largest-corporations-in-2013-the-chinese-are-rising/.
13. The complex interrelationship between offshoring and migration was explored in "Bridges and Barriers: Globalisation and the Mobility of Work and Workers," *Work Organisation, Labor and Globalisation* 6/2 (Fall 2012) available at http://analytica.metapress.com/content/j821245873x1/?p=0cc035504d50467cb90956c6d4312605&pi=0.

1. What Will We Do?

This essay was originally published in *Monthly Review* 57/8 (January 2006).

1. See http://www.hindubooks.org/sudheer_birodkar/hindu_history/castejati-varna.html, 2005.
2. Gøsta Esping-Anderson, *The Three Worlds of Welfare Capitalism* (Cambridge: Polity Press, 1990).
3. I am indebted to Markus Promberger for pointing out the historical importance of occupationally defined elites in the German trade union movement. E-mail correspondence, May 31, 2005.
4. For a more detailed explication of the commodification process, see Ursula Huws, *The Making of a Cybertariat: Virtual Work in a Real World* (New York: Monthly Review Press, 2003).
5. Peter Doeringer and Michael Piore, *Internal Labor Markets and Manpower Analysis* (Lanham, MD: Lexington Books, 1971).
6. Jill Rubery and Frank Wilkinson, *Labour Market Structure, Industrial Organisation and Low Pay* (Cambridge: Cambridge University Press, 1982).
7. David Coates, *Models of Capitalism: Growth and Stagnation in the Modern Era* (Cambridge: Polity Press, 2000).
8. Adapted from Rosemary Crompton and Kay Sanderson, *Gendered Jobs and Social Change* (London: Unwin Hyman, 1990).
9. This article was written before the 2007–8 financial crisis. Since then, we have, of course, seen an enormous extension both of

unemployment and of casualization across the developed world, but still taking a different character in different national contexts.

10. Hans Georg Zilian, "Welfare and Employment Flexibility within the New Labour Market," paper presented at the Workshop on "Labour and Welfare in Europe in the Information Economy: Is There a Danger of Digital Divide?" LAW (Labour@Welfare) Project, March 1, 2005, Brussels.
11. See http://info.worldbank.org/etools/kam2005/index.htm.
12. I am indebted to Yigit Kargin for bringing this to my attention.
13. See http://europa.eu.int/scadplus/leg/en/cha/c11053.htm.
14. Since this article was written, Romania and Bulgaria have both joined the EU, as has Croatia.
15. Ursula Huws, Jörg Flecker, and Simone Dahlmann, *Outsourcing of ICT and Related Services in the EU*, Research Report for the European Monitoring Centre for Change, European Foundation for the Improvement of Living and Working Conditions, Dublin, December 2004. Available online at: http://www.eurofound.europa.eu/publications/htmlfiles/ef04137.htm.

2. Fixed, Footloose, or Fractured

This essay was originally published in *Monthly Review* 57/10 (March 2006).

1. Paul Baran and Paul Sweezy, *Monopoly Capital: An Essay on the American Economic and Social Order* (New York: Monthly Review Press, 1966).
2. F. Froebel, J. Heinrichs, and O. Krey, *The New International Division of Labor* (Cambridge: Cambridge University Press, 1979).
3. See, for instance, Women Working Worldwide, *Common Interests: Women Organising in Global Electronics* (London: Women Working Worldwide, 1991).
4. Ursula Huws, *The Making of a Cybertariat: Virtual Work in a Real World* (New York: Monthly Review Press, 2003; and London: Merlin Books, 2003).
5. Quoted in *The Ecoonomist:* "A Survey of India's Economy," June 2, 2001.
6. Since this article was originally written, the global division of labor has developed much further, with new destinations coming into play, for instance in Eastern Europe and the Middle East, and some evidence of "backsourcing," whereby companies that originally outsourced abroad are now, having shaken out the trade unions and

introduced new working practices, moving work back to destinations in the developed world, for instance to southern states in the United States.

7. Ursula Huws, ed., *When Work Takes Flight: Research Results from the EMERGENCE Project*, IES Report 397, Institute for Employment Studies, Brighton, UK, 2003.
8. Ursula Huws and J. Flecker, eds., *Asian EMERGENCE: The World's Back Office?*, IES Report 409, Institute for Employment Studies, Brighton, UK, 2004.

3. Begging and Bragging

1. This chapter was first written as my inaugural lecture as Professor of International Labor Studies at London Metropolitan University, delivered 7 June 2006 at the university's Graduate Centre.
2. "Quango" is UK bureaucratese for "quasi-autonomous non-governmental organization."
3. Richard Florida, *The Rise of the Creative Class and How It Is Transforming Work, Leisure, Community and Everyday Life* (New York: Basic Books, 2002).
4. Tsugio Makimoto and David Manners, *Digital Nomad* (Chichester: John Wiley, 1997).
5. Robert B. Reich, *The Work of Nations* (New York: Vintage Books, 1991).
6. Charles Handy, *The Age of Unreason* (London: Hutchinson, 1989).
7. Since this was written, the Research Assessment (RAE) has been replaced in the UK by the even more arcane Research Excellence Framework (REF) in which scores for "excellence" (demonstrated by the quantity of articles published in high-ranked journals) are accompanied by scores for "impact."
8. Max Weber, *The Puritan Ethic and the Spirit of Capitalism,* quoted in Sam Whimster, *The Essential Weber* (London: Routledge, 2004).
9. Lee Comer, *Wedlocked Women* (Leeds, UK: Feminist Books, 1974).
10. Liz Heron, *Truth, Dare or Promise: Girls Growing up in the Fifties* (London: Virago Press, 1985).
11. Sandra Allen, Lee Sanders, and Jan Wallis, eds., *Conditions of Illusion: Papers from the Women's Movement* (Leeds, UK: Feminist Books, 1974).
12. Karl Marx's words, "The call to abandon their illusions about their conditions is a call to abandon a condition which requires illusions," are quoted on the title page of *Conditions of Illusion*.

13. London Metropolitan University, where this lecture was given, was formed from an amalgamation of London Guildhall University and the University of North London, formerly the Polytechnic of North London, where I taught in the early 1990s.
14. This was a project funded by the European Commission to develop ethical and professional guidelines for social research, concluded in 2004. See http://www.respectproject.org for more information.
15. The first time I wrote about this was in a paper for the Conference of Socialist Economics Microprocessors Group, written in 1978 and titled "New Technology and Domestic Labor," and since published as Ursula Huws, *The Making of a Cybertariat: Virtual Work in a Real World* (New York: Monthly Review Press, 2003), 24–34.
16. See, for instance, Arnold Reidmann, Harald Bielenski, Teresa Szczurowska, and Alexandra Wagner, *Working Time and Worklife Balance in European Companies* (Dublin: European Foundation for the Improvement of Living and Working Conditions, 2006).
17. Janice Newson and Heather Menzies, "Findings From the Time, Technology and Academic Work" study, presented at the Gender, Work and Organization Conference, Keele University, UK, 22–24 June 2005.
18. Virginia Woolf, *A Room of One's Own* (London: Hogarth Press, 1929).
19. Q. Hoare and G. N. Smith, eds., "The Intellectuals," in *Selections from the Prison Notebooks* (New York: International Publishers, 1971). 3–23. Originally published as Antonio Gramsci, *Gli intellettuali e l'organizzazione della cultura*, ed. F. Platone (Turin: Nuovo Universale Einaudi, 1949).
20. Pierre Bourdieu, *Contre-feux 2* (Paris: Raisons d'Agir, 2001).

4. The Globalization of Labor and the Role of National Governments

1. This essay draws on a series of reports and articles I wrote in 2009–10, most notably a chapter originally published as "This Historical Roots of the Concept of the Value Chain," in Huws et al., eds., *Value Chain Restructuring in Europe in a Global Economy.* See full cite in n. 20. This is discussed in more detail elsewhere in this book, in the chapter "Crisis as Capitalist Opportunity."
2. I. Wallerstein, *The Capitalist World Economy* (Cambridge: Cambridge University Press, 1979); M. Porter, *Competitive Advantage: Creating and Sustaining Superior Performance* (New York: Simon & Schuster, 1985); G. Gereffi, J. Humphrey, and T.

Sturgeon, "The Governance of Global Value Chains," *Review of International Political Economy* 12/1 (2005): 78–104.

3. J. H. Lorenzi, O. Pastré, and J. Toledano, *La Crise du XXème siècle* (Paris : Economica, Paris, 1980); Y. Morvan, ed., *L'Analyse de filière* (Paris: Economica, 1985); G. Schméder, "Les Interprétations technologiques de la crise," *Critique de l'économie politique* 26–27 (June 1984): 41–52.
4. M. Castells, *The Rise of the Network Society* (Oxford: Blackwell Publishers, 1996).
5. Adam Smith, *An Inquiry into the Nature and Causes of the Wealth of Nations,* 1776 available at http://www.adamsmith.org/smith/won-b1-intro.htm.
6. Karl Marx, *Capital,* 1867, available at http://www.marxists.org/archive/marx/works/1867-c1.
7. David Ricardo, *The Principles of Political Economy and Taxation,* 1817, available at http://socserv2.socsci.mcmaster.ca/econ/ugcm/3ll3/ricardo/prin/index.html.
8. François Quesnay, *Tableau Économique*, 1758, "third edition," as reprinted in M. Kuczynsi and R. L. Meek, eds., *Quesnay's Tableau Économique* (New York: A. M. Kelley, 1972). Summarized at http://cepa.newschool.edu/het/essays/youth/tableauoverview.htm#summary.
9. Smith, *An Inquiry into the Nature and Causes of the Wealth of Nations,* Book 1, chap. 1.
10. Ibid., Book 1, chap. 4.
11. Ibid.
12. Ricardo, *The Principles of Political Economy and Taxation*, chap. 7.
13. Smith, *An Inquiry into the Nature and Causes of the Wealth of Nations,* Book 1, chap. 10, pt. 2.
14. Karl Marx, *Economic Works of Karl Marx 1861–1864, vol.* 2, *Capitalist Production as the Production of Surplus Value*, available at http://www.marxists.org/archive/marx/works/1864/economic/ch02b.htm. Emphasis in Marx's original.
15. W. F. Taylor, *The Principles of Scientific Management* (New York: Harper Bros, 1911). Available at http://www.fordham.edu/halsall/mod/1911taylor.html (introduction), and http://www.marxists.org/reference/subject/economics/taylor/principles/ch02.htm.
16. H. Braverman, *Labor and Monopoly Capital: The Degradation of Work in the Twentieth Century* (New York: Monthly Review Press, 1974).
17. Taylor, *The Principles of Scientific Management,* chap. 2.

18. M. Polanyi, *Personal Knowledge: Towards a Post-Critical Philosophy* (1958; repr., London: Routledge, 1998).
19. Ursula Huws, *The Making of a Cybertariat: Virtual Work in a Real World* (New York: Monthly Review Press, 2003).
20. Ursula Huws, S. Dahlmann, J. Flecker, U. Holtgrewe, A. Schönauer, M. Ramioul, and K. Geurts, *Value Chain Restructuring in Europe in a Global Economy* (Leuven, Belg.: Higher Institute of Labor Studies, K.U. Leuven, 2009).
21. K. Ohmae, *The Borderless World: Power and Strategy in the Interlinked World Economy* (London: HarperCollins, 1990), 18.
22. R. Cox, "Global Perestroika," in *New World Order? Socialist Register*, ed. R. Miliband and L. Panitch (London: Merlin Press, 1992), 27.
23. L. Panitch, "Globalization and the State," in *The Globalization Decade*, ed. L. Panitch, C. Leys, A. Zuege, and M. Konings (London: Merlin, 2004), 1.
24. D. Coates, *Models of Capitalism: Growth and Stagnation in the Modern Era* (Cambridge: Polity Press, 2000), 225.
25. For the case of Colombia, see A. Weiss, "Global Forces and National Institutions: The Shaping of Call Centre Employment in Colombia," *Work Organization, Labor and Globalization* 1/2 (2007):131–54.
26. For D. Coates, see *Models of Capitalism: Growth and Stagnation in the Modern Era*; and *Models of Capitalism: Debating Strengths and Weaknesses*, vol. 1 (Cheltenham and Camberley: Edward Elgar, 2002); P. A. Hall and D. Soskice, *Varieties of Capitalism* (Oxford: Oxford University Press, 2001).
27. G. Esping-Andersen, *The Three Worlds of Welfare Capitalism* (Cambridge: Polity Press, 1990).

5. Expression and Expropriation

This essay was originally published in *Ephemera* 10/3–4 (2010).

1. See Ursula Huws, "The Spark in the Engine: Creative Workers in a Global Economy," *Work Organization, Labor and Globalization* 1/1 (2006): 1–12.
2. This project was funded under the European Commission's 6th Framework Program as an integrated project, under the leadership of Monique Ramioul, at the Higher Institute of Labor Studies of the Catholic University of Leuven, with 17 partner institutes in 14 EU countries. See http://www.worksproject.be for further information.
3. J. Flecker, U. Holtgrewe, A. Schönauer, W. Dunkel, and P. Meil, *Restructuring Across Value Chains and Changes in Work and*

Employment: Case Study Evidence from the Clothing, Food, IT and Public Sectors, WORKS Project, Higher Institute of Labor Studies, K.U. Leuven (Leuven: HIVA, 2008).

4. G. Valenduc, P. Vendramin, B.-J. Krings, and L. Nierling, *Occupational Case Studies: Synthesis Report and Comparative Analysis,* WORKS Project, Higher Institute of Labor Studies, K.U. Leuven (Leuven: HIVA, 2007).
5. J. Flecker, U. Holtgrewe, A. Schönauer, and S. Gavroglou, *Value Chain Restructuring and Company Strategies to Reach Flexibility,* WORKS Project, Higher Institute of Labor Studies, K.U. Leuven (Leuven: HIVA, 2009); B.-J. Krings, L. Nierling, M. Pedaci, and M. Piersanti, *Working Time, Gender, Work-Life Balance*, WORKS Project, Higher Institute of Labor Studies, K.U. Leuven (Leuven: HIVA, 2009); U. Huws, S. Dahlmann, J. Flecker, U. Holtgrewe, A.Schönauer, M. Ramioul, and K. Geurts, *Value Chain Restructuring in Europe in a Global Economy,* Higher Institute of Labor Studies, K. U. Leuven (Leuven: HIVA, 2009).
6. N. Greenan, E. Kalugina, and E. Walkowiak, "European Working Conditions Survey," in *The Transformation of Work? A Quantitative Evaluation of the Shape of Employment in Europe,* ed. Birindelli et al., WORKS Project, Higher Institute of Labor Studies, K.U. Leuven (Leuven: HIVA, 2007).
7. M. Ramioul and B. De Vroom, *Global Value Chain Restructuring and the Use of Knowledge and Skills,* WORKS Project, Higher Institute of Labor Studies, K. U. Leuven (Leuven: HIVA, 2009).
8. P. Meil, P. Tengblad, and P. Docherty, *Value Chain Restructuring and Industrial Relations: The Role of Workplace Representation in Changing Conditions of Employment and Work*, WORKS Project, Higher Institute of Labor Studies, K.U. Leuven (Leuven: HIVA, 2009), 65, 69.
9. S. Dahlmann, *Organizational Case Study on IT Service Providers in Public Administration—UK,* internal working paper, WORKS Project, 2007; S. Dahlmann (2008), "The End of the Road: No More Walking in Dead Men's Shoes," *Work Organization, Labor and Globalization* 2/2 (2008): 148–61.
10. H. Braverman, *Labor and Monopoly Capital* (New York: Monthly Review Press, 1974), 85–121.
11. F. W. Taylor, *The Principles of Scientific Management* (New York: W. W. Norton, 1911), available at http://www.marxists.org/reference/subject/.../taylor/index.htm.

12. Braverman, *Labor and Monopoly Capital*, 124–37.
13. M. Hales, *Living Think Work: Where Do Labor Processes Come From?* (London: CSE Books, 1980).
14. Karl Marx, *Grundrisse* (Harmondsworth: Penguin, 1973), available at http://www.marxists.org/archive/marx/works/1857/grundrisse/ch12.htm#p610.
15. See S. Sayers, "Creative Activity and Alienation in Hegel and Marx," *Historical Materialism* 11/1: 107–28.
16. M. Muchnik, *Dress Designers or Fashion Artists? Occupational Case Study on Designers in Clothing in France*, WORKS Project working document, Fondation Travail Universitaire, University of Namur, May 2007.
17. Quoted in G. Valenduc, P. Vendramin, M. Pedaci, and M. Piersanti, *Changing Careers and Trajectories: How Individuals Cope with Organizational Change and Restructuring,* WORKS Project, Higher Institute of Labor Studies, K. U. Leuven (Leuven: HIVA, 2009), 36.
18. Krings et al., *Working Time, Gender, Work-Life Balance*, 85.
19. Ramioul and De Vroom, *Global Value Chain Restructuring and the Use of Knowledge and Skills,* 85.
20. For the "occupational case studies" on R&D in the IT industry, four case studies were carried out, in Norway, Austria, Germany, and France, each involving 7–10 interviews. These complemented "organizational case studies" of value chain restructuring in the industry.
21. Flecker et al., *Restructuring Across Value Chains and Changes in Work and Employment,* 24.
22. Krings et al., *Working Time, Gender, Work-Life Balance*, 30.
23. For the "occupational case studies" of fashion designers, interviews were carried out in France, Germany and Portugal with 22 designers in nine firms, of whom 17 were women and five men, aged between 27 and 53.
24. G. Valenduc, P. Vendramin, B.-J. Krings, and L. Nierling, *Occupational Case Studies: Synthesis Report and Comparative Analysis,* WORKS Project, Higher Institute of Labor Studies, K.U. Leuven (Leuven: HIVA, 2007), 41.
25. Ramioul and De Vroom, *Global Value Chain Restructuring and the Use of Knowledge and Skills,* 45.
26. Valenduc et al., *Occupational Case Studies: Synthesis Report and Comparative Analysis,* 86.
27. Ibid., 86.

28. M. Ramioul and U. Huws, "The Snowball Effect: Global Sourcing as an Accelerator of Economic Globalization," *Journal of Architectural and Planning Research* 26/4 (2009): 327–42.
29. J. Flecker, U. Holtgrewe, A. Schönauer, and S. Gavroglou, *Value Chain Restructuring and Company Strategies to Reach Flexibility*, WORKS Project, Higher Institute of Labor Studies, K.U. Leuven (Leuven: HIVA, 2009).
30. There is no space to do more than list these here. Readers who are interested in finding out more can find a number of relevant articles in *Work Organization, Labor and Globalization*, which can be accessed online at http://analytica.metapress.com.
31. U. Huws, S. Dahlmann, J. Flecker, U. Holtgrewe, A. Schönauer, M. Ramioul, and K. Geurts, *Value Chain Restructuring in Europe in a Global Economy*, Higher Institute of Labor Studies, K.U. Leuven (Leuven: HIVA, 2009).
32. A. K. Damarin, "The Network-Organized Labor Process: Control and Autonomy in Web Production Work," paper presented at the International Labor Process Conference, Rutgers University, New Brunswick, NJ, March 2010, 1.
33. P. B. Doeringer and M. J. Piore, *Internal Labor Markets and Manpower Analysis* (Lexington, MA: D.C. Heath and Company, 1971).
34. H. Braverman, *Labor and Monopoly Capital* (New York: Monthly Review Press, 1974).
35. M. Burawoy, *Manufacturing Consent* (Chicago: University of Chicago Press, 1979).
36. M. Cooley, *Architect or Bee?* (Boston: South End Press, 1999).
37. H. Beynon, *Working for Ford* (Wakefield, UK: E. P. Publishing, 1975).
38. L. Schumaker, "Immaterial Fordism: The Paradox of Game Industry Labor," *Work Organization, Labor and Globalization* 1/1 (2006): 144–55.
39. See C. Leys, *Market-Driven Politics: Neoliberal Democracy and the Public Interest* (London: Verso, 2003); and U. Huws, "The New Gold Rush: The New Multinationals and the Commodification of Public Sector Work," *Work Organization, Labor and Globalization* 2/2 (2008).
40. Damarin, "The Network-Organized Labor Process."
41. J. Lave and E. Wenger, *Situated Learning: Legitimate Peripheral Participation* (Cambridge: Cambridge University Press, 1991).

42. "Planning for the Sequel: How Pixar's Leaders Want to Make Their Creative Powerhouse Outlast Them," *The Economist*, June 17, 2010.
43. See A. F. Steinko, "Rethinking Progressive and Conservative Values: Spain's New Economy Workers and Their Values," *Work Organization, Labor and Globalization* 1/1 (2006).
44. But see Mosco and McKercher, "Getting the Message: Communications Workers in Global Value Chains," *Work Organization, Labor and Globalization* 4/2 (2010), for more positive evidence.
45. U. Huws, "Defragmenting: Towards a Critical Understanding of the New Global Division of Labor," *Work Organization, Labor and Globalization* 1/2 (2007).
46. Ramioul and De Vroom, *Global Value Chain Restructuring and the Use of Knowledge and Skills.*
47. P. D'Cruz and E. Noronha, "Experiencing Depersonalized Bullying: A Study of Indian Call-Centre Agents," *Work Organization, Labor and Globalization* 3/1(2009): 24–46.
48. P. Bramming, O. Sørensen, and P. Hasle, "In Spite of Everything: Professionalism as Mass Customized Bureaucratic Production in a Danish Government Call Centre," *Work Organization, Labor and Globalization* 3/1 (2009): 114–30.

6. Crisis as Capitalist Opportunity

This essay was originally published in *Socialist Register* (2012).

1. Or, perhaps more precisely, it could be said that uncommodified use values are being transformed into commodified use values, giving them exchange value in the market.
2. See Claude Serfarti, "Transnational Organisations as Financial Groups," in *Work Organization, Labour and Globalisation* 5/1, for an interesting discussion of the convergence between non-financial and financial TNCs.
3. UNCTAD, *World Development Report*, 2008, 3.
4. Ibid., 4.
5. Ibid., xv–xvi.
6. Ibid., 4.
7. For instance, when it was introduced during the late 1990s in the IT industry for labor-intensive programming tasks such as converting European company accounting systems to cope with the introduction of the euro or averting the catastrophes it was predicted would be caused by the "millennium bug."

8. I have written extensively elsewhere about the long development of this new global division of labor from the 1970s on in, for instance, Ursula Huws, *The Making of a Cybertariat* (New York: Monthly Review Press, 2003); Huws, "Fixed, Footloose or Fractured: Work, Identity, and the Spatial Division of Labor," in *Monthly Review* 57/10 (March 2006); Huws and J. Flecker, *Asian Emergence: The World's Back Office?*, IES Report 419 (Brighton: Institute for Employment Studies, 2005).
9. This process is described in more detail in Huws (2006), "The Restructuring of Global Value Chains and the Creation of a Cybertariat," in *Global Corporate Power: Global Corporate Power: (Re)integrating companies into International Political Economy*, ed. Christopher May, International Political Economy Yearbook, vol. 15 (Boulder, CO: Lynne Rienner Publishers, 2006), 65–84.
10. D. Julius, *Public Services Industry Review* (London: Department for Business Enterprise and Regulatory Reform, 2008).
11. Including post and telecommunications, energy and water networks, formerly publicly-owned airlines, state-owned banks, and public housing stock.
12. OECD data quoted in "A Special Report on the Future of the State," *The Economist,* March 19, 2011, 4.
13. IMF data, quoted in ibid., 5.
14. G. Esping-Anderson, *The Three Worlds of Welfare Capitalism* (Princeton: Princeton University Press, 1990).
15. Huws, "Move Over Brother," *New Socialist,* January 1985.
16. Subsequently, this process culminated in the 2006 Services Directive (2006/123), which came into force on 28 December 2009, effectively removing any national barriers within the EU to companies wishing to tender for public services.
17. Again, this set the scene for further liberalization of international trade in services under the GATS. In the words of the WTO: "The Uruguay Round was on the beginning. GATS requires more negotiations which began in early 2000 and are now part of the Doha Development Agenda. The goal is to take the liberalization process further by increasing the level of commitments in schedules." *Understanding the WTO: The Agreements,* available at http://www.wto.org/english/thewto_e/whatis_e/tif_e/agrm6_e.htm.
18. B. Jessop, *The Future of the Capitalist State* (Oxford: Polity Press, 2002).
19. Since the crisis, austerity measures have taken a heavy toll on the numbers and quality of public sector jobs.

20. Union density is significantly higher among public sector workers than their private sector counterparts in every European country other than Belgium. V. Glassner, *The Public Sector in the Crisis*, Working Paper 2010.07 (Brussels: European Trade Union Institute, 2010), 15.
21. I have written at greater length about this process in, for instance, Huws, *The Making of a Cybertariat*; and Huws, "The New Gold Rush," *Work Organisation, Labour and Globalisation* 2/2 (2008).
22. For a detailed anatomization, see C. Leys and S. Player, *Confuse and Conceal: The NHS and Independent Sector Treatment Centers* (London: Merlin, 2008).
23. See D. Whitfield, "Marketisation of Legal Services," *Legal Action*, March 2007.
24. C. Leys, *Market-Driven Politics* (London: Verso, 2003).
25. A. Hochschild, *The Managed Heart: The Commercialization of Human Feeling* (Berkeley: University of California Press, 1983).
26. The question is sometimes raised whether there is any improvement in the quality of services that have been standardized, commodified, and outsourced. The implication is that if this is the case then the benefits to service users may outweigh any disadvantages to workers. In fact, it is extremely difficult to make such comparisons for a number of reasons. First, restructuring is often introduced in situations in which services are already deteriorating because of spending cuts. Second, the change processes associated with commodification make it difficult to compare like with like. Third, the obsessive focus on quantitative indicators that is an essential underpinning of commodification renders invisible many of the qualitative changes that may be experienced negatively by service users. Nevertheless, there is a considerable body of research (for example, by Leys and Pollock, Leys and Player, and Whitfield) that suggests there is a deterioration. It is perhaps no accident that John Hutton, Secretary of State for Business Enterprise and Regulatory Reform in the New Labour Government in 2008, stopped even arguing that the main advantage of outsourcing was to bring efficiency savings. The Public Services Industry, he said, should be encouraged because "there is significant export potential in this growth industry. Encouraging and assisting UK firms to make the most of these opportunities will generate substantial benefits not only for UK firms but also for the UK economy. The *Review* concludes that the best way that government can support the PSI abroad is

through maintaining a competitive framework for public services which fosters a dynamic and thriving PSI in the UK." Introduction to D. Julius, *Public Services Industry Review* (London: Department for Business Enterprise and Regulatory Reform, 2008).

27. The International Organization for Standardization, which has 2,700 technical committees, subcommittees, and working groups, sets international technical standards for a large range of different industrial processes. The existence of these standards means that it is possible to trade with, or outsource to, an ISO-certified company in the confidence that the outputs will be predictable and standardized, removing the need for detailed supervision, in just the same way that, for instance, electrical standards make it possible to plug an appliance into a standard socket in the confidence that it will function correctly.
28. ISO, *ISO Annual Report*, 2010 (Geneva: International Standardization Organization, 2010).
29 In this case, see http://www.certificationskit.com/cisco-certification/cisco-certification-salary-statistics/.
30. B. Caraway, "Online Labor Markets: An Enquiry into oDesk Providers," *Work Organisation, Labour and Globalisation* 4/2 (2010): 111–25.
31. See http://www.trainsignaltraining.com/microsoft-performance-based-testing.
32. I have written in greater depth about the changing occupational identities of IT workers in the context of globalization in Huws, "New Forms of Work; New Occupational Identities," in *Interrogating the "New Economy": Restructuring Work in the 21st Century*, ed. N. Pupo and M Thomas (Peterborough, Ont.: Broadview Press, 2010).
33. See C. Dixon, "The Reformatting of State Control in Vietnam," *Work Organisation, Labour and Globalisation* 2/2 (2008): 101–18.
34. See http://www.serco.com/instituteresource/about/index.asp.
35. C. Leys and S. Player, *The Plot Against the NHS* (London: Merlin, 2011).
36. For a detailed description of the impact on workers' skills on the "call-centerization" of the Danish tax system, see Bramming, Sørensen, and Hasle, "In Spite of Everything: Professionalism as Mass Customized Bureaucratic Production in a Danish Government Call Center," *Work Organization, Labour and Globalisation* 3/1 (2009): 114–30.
37. See P. Meil, P. Tengblad, and P. Docherty, *Value Chain Restructuring and Industrial Relations—The Role of Workplace Representation in*

Changing Conditions of Employment and Work, WORKS Project, Higher Institute of Labor Studies, K.U. Leuven (Leuven: HIVA, 2009).

38. S. Dahlmann, "The End of the Road, No More Walking in Dead Men's Shoes: IT Professionals' Experiences of Being Outsourced to the Private Sector," *Work Organisation, Labour and Globalisation* 2/2(2008): 148–61.
39. This case study is described in greater detail in ibid.
40. H. Reed, *The Shrinking State: Why the Rush to Outsource Threatens Our Public Services* (London: A Report for Unite by Landman Economics, 2011), 13.
41. Ibid., 18.
42. Julius.
43. S. Lister, "NHS Is World's Biggest Employer after Indian Rail and Chinese Army," London *Times*, March 20, 2004, http://www.timesonline.co.uk/tol/news/uk/health/article1050197.ece.
44. A. Bawden, "Suffolk Council Plans to Outsource Virtually All Services," *The Guardian*, September 22, 2010, http://www.guardian.co.uk/society/2010/sep/22/suffolk-county-council-outsource-services.
45. D. Whitfield, *Future Shape of the Council: The Flaws in Barnet's Commissioning and Procurement Policy* (London: European Services Strategy Unit, 2008).
46. "There Goes Everybody," *The Economist*, July 8, 2010, http://www.economist.com/node/16541692?story_id=16541692.
47. Cabinet Office, *Modernising Commissioning: Increasing the Role of Charities, Social Enterprises, Mutuals and Co-Operatives in Public Service Delivery*, 2010, 5. Emphasis in the original.
48. Aga Khan Development Network, "Upgrading Nursing Studies: Strengthening the Health-Care System in Tanzania," http://www.akdn.org/publications/2007_akf_tanzania_nursing.pdf.
49. B. Neilson, "Guijing Migrant Village," *Transit Labor* 2 (December 2010): 33–35.

7. The Underpinnings of Class in the Digital Age

This essay was originally published in *Socialist Register* (2014), 80–107.

1. M. Hardt and A. Negri, *Multitude: War and Democracy in the Age of Empire* (New York: Penguin, 2004); G. Standing, *Precariat: The New Dangerous Class* (London and New York: Bloomsbury, 2011).
2. Hardt and Negri, *Multitude*; T. Terranova, "Free Labor: Producing Culture for the Digital Economy," *Social Text* 18/2) (2000): 33–58.

3. See, for instance, M. Andrejevic, "Exploiting YouTube: Contradictions of User-Generated Labor," in *The YouTube Reader*, ed. P. Snickers and P. Vonderau (Stockholm: National Library of Sweden, 2009); A. Arvidsson and E. Colleoni, "Value in Informational Capitalism and on the Internet," *The Information Society* 28/3 (2012): 135–50; J. Banks and S. Humphreys, "The Labor of User Co-Creators," *Convergence* 14/4 (2008): 401–18; C. Fuchs, "Labor in Informational Capitalism and on the Internet," *The Information Society* 26/3 (2010): 179–96; C. Fuchs, "With or Without Marx? With or Without Capitalism? A Rejoinder to Adam Arvidsson and Eleanor Colleoni," *Triple C* 10/2 (2012): 633–45; D. Hesmondhalgh, "User-Generated Content, Free Labor and the Cultural Industries," *Ephemera* 10/3–4 (2011): 267–84; A. Ross, "On the Digital Labor Question," in *The Internet as Playground and Factory*, ed. T. Scholz (New York: Routledge, 2012); and Tiziana Terranova, "Free Labor," in Scholz, *Internet as Playground and Factory*.
4. J. Kücklich, "Precarious Playbour: Modders and the Digital Games Industry," *The Fibreculture Journal* 5 (2005).
5. Alvin Toffler coined this term in his 1980 book *The Third Wave*, published by Bantam Books. It has since been taken up by a number of other writers working in a Marxist framework, including Christian Fuchs and Ed Comer.
6. John Banks and Sal Humphreys, "The Labor of User Co-Creators," using a term derived from C. K. Prahalad and V. Ramaswamy, "Co-Opting Customer Competence," *Harvard Business Review*, January–February 2000.
7. A term coined by Tiziana Terranova in her influential article, "Free Labor."
8. U. Huws, "Crisis as Capitalist Opportunity: The New Accumulation through Public Service Commodification," *Socialist Register* (2012): 64–84.
9. U. Huws, "Domestic Technology: Liberator or Enslaver?," in *The Making of a Cybertariat: Virtual Work in a Real World* (New York: Monthly Review Press, 2003), 35–41.
10. U. Huws, "Material World: The Myth of the Weightless Economy," *Socialist Register* (1999): 29–56.
11. UNCTAD, *World Investment Report*, Geneva, 2008.
12. According to UNCTAD, 60 percent of manufacturing TNCs were planning to increase their FDI in the next year, compared with 45

percent of firms in the primary sector and 43 percent of those in services. See *World Investment Report*, 2012, 19.

13. Karl Marx, *Grundrisse*, "Chapter on Money," Part 2, available at http://www.marxists.org.
14. D. W. Smythe, "Communications: Blindspot of Western Marxism," *Canadian Journal of Political and Social Theory* 1/3 (1977): 1–27.
15. Christian Fuchs, "Dallas Smythe Today—The Audience Commodity, the Digital *Labor* Debate, Marxist Political Economy and Critical Theory. Prolegomena to a Digital *Labor* Theory of Value," *Triple C* 10/2 (2012): 692–740.
16. Dallas W. Smythe, "On the Audience Commodity and Its Work," in *Media and Cultural Studies*, ed. M. G. Duncan and D. M. Kellner (Malden, MA: Blackwell, 1981), 233.
17. A. Hearn, "Structuring Feeling: Web 2.0, Online Ranking and Rating, and the Digital 'Reputation' Economy," *Ephemera* 10/3–4 (2010): 421–38.
18. C. Morini and A. Fumagalli, "Life Put to Work: Towards a Life Theory of Value," *Ephemera* 10/3–4 (2010): 234–52.
19. Karl Marx, *Capital*, chap. 1, available at http://www.marxists.org.
20. Huws, *Making of a Cybertariat*, 17.
21. This point is made a little differently in a discussion of the distinction between productive and unproductive labor by Marx in *Capital*, chap. 4.
22. Except in some special circumstances, such as when workers are paid to go on Facebook and click "Like" on commercial websites in the "pay per click" model. But here they are not employed by Facebook but by companies linked to these commercial websites that have some commodity to sell, so they should more accurately be regarded as belonging to the value chain of these commodity-producing companies.
23. Arvidsson and Colleoni, "Value in Informational Capitalism."
24. Arvidsson and Colleoni, ibid.
25. "All Eyes on the Sharing Economy," *The Economist*, 9 March 2013.
26. I am indebted to Kaire Holts for drawing my attention to this explanation of the business model of reCAPTCHA by its originator, who also founded Duolingo, available at http://www.willhambly.com. See also the related video, available at http://www.inmyinnovation.com.
27. I have discussed the concept of the "business function" and its relation to Marxist analysis in several publications. See, for instance, U. Huws, "The Restructuring of Global Value Chains and the

Creation of a Cybertariat," in *Global Corporate Power: (Re)integrating Companies into International Political Economy*, ed. Christopher May, International Political Economy Yearbook, vol. 15 (Boulder, CO: Lynne Rienner Publishers, 2006), 65–84; and U. Huws, "The Emergence of EMERGENCE: The Challenge of Designing Research on the New International Division of Labor," *Work Organisation, Labour and Globalisation* 1/2 (2007): 20–35.

28. I have analyzed the relationship of creative *labor* to capital elsewhere. See, for instance, U. Huws, "Expression and Expropriation: The Dialectics of Autonomy and Control in Creative Labor," *Ephemera* 10/3–4 (2010).
29. Kittur et al., "The Future of Crowd Work," 2013, available at http://hci.stanford.edu.
30. K. Holts, "Towards a Taxonomy of Virtual Work," Hertfordshire Business School Working Paper, 2013.
31. Marx, *Grundrisse*, Notebook 5. It should be noted that this interpretation of this passage is disputed. Marx is often considered to be making a special exception of transport workers, perhaps because they were a group with strong potential trade union organization—a potential that was more than realized in the twentieth century when transport workers played a key role in industrial action. It is my view that his argument applies equally to other forms of labor involved in getting products to market, many of which were inconceivable at the time when he was writing.
32. Terranova, "Free Labor."
33. B. Weinbaum and A. Bridges, "The Other Side of the Paycheck: Monopoly Capital and the Structure of Consumption," *Monthly Review* 28/3 (1976).
34. See, for instance, Huws, "Domestic Technology."
35. See Karl Marx, *Economic Manuscripts*, chap. 4, available at http://www.marxists.org.
36. I use the term "externalizing" here to refer to the ways in which employers increase the productivity of paid staff by transferring some or all of their unpaid tasks to unpaid consumers in the form of self-service, whether through the operation of machines such as ATMs or self-service supermarket or online activities such as booking tickets, filling in tax returns, or ordering goods.
37. Marx, *Economic Manuscripts*, chap. 2.
38. A. Ross, "In Search of the Lost Paycheck," in Scholz, *Internet as Playground and Factory*, 15.

39. I have anatomized these in greater detail in Huws, "Expression and Expropriation," 504–21.
40. Marx, "Productive and Unproductive Labor," in *Economic Manuscripts*.
41. See, for instance, R. Perlin, *Intern Nation: How to Earn Nothing and Learn Little in the Brave New Economy* (London: Verso, 2011).
42. I have written more extensively about this in U. Huws, "The Reproduction of Difference: Gender and the Global Division of Labor," *Work Organisation, Labour and Globalisation* 6/1 (2012): 1–10.
43. Karl Marx, "Division of Labor and Forms of Property—Tribal, Ancient, Feudal," Part 1-A, *The German Ideology*, 1845, available at http://www.marxists.org.
44. Friedrich Engels, *On Marx's Capital* (1877; Moscow: Progress Publishers, 1956), 89.
45. For more on this, see my blog post on "Hunger in a Supermarketocracy," available at http://ursulahuws.wordpress.com. In the UK, according to HM Revenue and Customs, "the numbers of families without children receiving Working Tax Credits-only has risen over time, almost doubling from 235,000 in April 2004 to around 455,000 in April 2009 and now at just over 580,000 in April 2012" and "the numbers of families benefiting from the childcare element has consistently risen over time, from 318,000 in April 2004 to around 493,000 in April 2011." By this date tax credits (paid to workers in employment) already accounted for 27 percent of all benefit spending—by far the largest single component. By comparison Job-Seekers Allowance (paid to the unemployed) accounted for only 4 percent. In the United States, similarly, many large companies rely on government-provided benefits, such as food stamps and Medicaid, to subsidize below-subsistence wages. For instance, Walmart employees are estimated to receive $2.66 billion in government assistance every year, or about $420,000 per store. See HM Revenue and Customs, Child and Working Tax Credits Statistics, Office of National Statistics, 2012; and Ryan, "Walmart: America's Real 'Welfare Queen,'" *Daily Kos*, 2012, available at http://www.dailykos.com.
46. See http://www.cleanclothes.org.

Index